HORROR ALMANAC

1970-2020

COMPLETE HORROR MOVIE STATISTICS

CONTENTS

Writers	Mario Bava, Guiseppe Zaccariello, Filippo Ottoni
Producers	Guiseppe Zaccariello
Directors	Mario Bava
Box Office	---
Awards	Sitges Catalonian International Film Festival – Best Special Effects

Main Cast	
Actor / Actress	**Screen Names**
Claudine Auger	Renata Donati
Luigi Pistilli	Alberto

Facts / More
Christopher Lee reportedly left the theater in protest during the film due to the level of violence.
Total Film ranked *A Bay of Blood* as one of their top 50 horror movies of all time.

THE DEVILS

Release Date	July 16, 1971
Budget	---
Studio	Russo Productions, Warner Bros.
Run Time	111 minutes (117 minutes restored version)
Sub-genre	History
Source / Inspiration	Urbain Grandier: A French Catholic priest who was burned at the stake in the 17th century after being convicted of witchcraft. The Devils of Loudun: Non-fiction novel by Aldous Huxley.
Writers	Ken Russell
Producers	Ken Russell, Robert H. Solo, Russo Productions
Directors	Ken Russell
Box Office	$11,000,000
Awards	Venice Film Festival – Best Foreign Film Italian National Syndicate of Film Journalists - Best Foreign Director National Board of Review, USA – Best Director

Main Cast	
Actor / Actress	**Screen Names**
Vanessa Redgrave	Sister Jeanne
Oliver Reed	Urbain Grandier

Facts / More
The Devils Is ranked the best horror movie of 1971.

1972

LAST HOUSE ON THE LEFT

Release Date	August 30, 1972
Budget	$87,000
Studio	Hallmark Releasing, American International Pictures
Run Time	84 minutes
Sub-genre	Thriller
Source / Inspiration	---
Writers	Wes Craven
Producers	Sean S. Cummingham
Directors	Wes Craven
Box Office	$3,100,000
Awards	---
Main Cast	

Actor / Actress	Screen Names
Sandra Peabody	Mari Collingwood
Lucy Grantham	Phyllis Stone
David Hess	Krug Stillo

Facts / More
Last House on the Left was the first film Wes Craven ever directed.

NON SI SEVIZIA UN PAPERINO [DON'T TORTURE A DUCKLING]

Release Date	September 29, 1972
Budget	---
Studio	Medusa Distribuzione
Run Time	102 minutes, 105 minutes, 108 minutes (depending on version)
Sub-genre	Mystery Thriller
Source / Inspiration	---
Writers	Lucio Fulci, Roberto Gianviti, Gianfranco Clerici
Producers	Renato Jaboni
Directors	Lucio Fulci
Box Office	ITL 1,101,461,000 (Italian Lira)
Awards	---
Main Cast	

Actor / Actress	Screen Names
Florinda Bolken	Maciara
Barbara Bouchet	Patrizia
Tomas Millan	Andrea Martelli
Facts / More	

Lucio Fulci shared that this was his favorite of the films he directed.

TALES FROM THE CRYPT

Release Date	March 8, 1972
Budget	£170.000
Studio	Cinerama Releasing Corporation, Amicus Productions, Metro Media Producers Corporation
Run Time	92 minutes
Sub-genre	Mystery
Source / Inspiration	Tales from the Crypt Comic (1950-1955) The Vault of Horror Comic (1950s)
Writers	Milton Subotsky
Producers	Milton Subotsky, Max Rosenberg
Directors	Freddie Francis
Box Office	$3,000,000
Awards	---

Main Cast	
Actor / Actress	**Screen Names**
Ralph Richardson	The Crypt Keeper
Geoffrey Bayldon	Guide
Joan Collins	Joanne Clayton
Facts / More	

Stephen King (*The Shining*) and George Romero (*Night of the Living Dead*) considered remaking this movie together, but instead they made *Creepshow* (1982) which is a completely different movie with similarities to *Tales from the Crypt*.

DELIVERANCE

Release Date	July 30, 1972 – August 18, 1972 (depending on location)
Budget	$2,000,000
Studio	Warner Bros.
Run Time	109 minutes
Sub-genre	Thriller

Source / Inspiration	Deliverance by James Dickey (novel)
Writers	James Dickey
Producers	John Boorman
Directors	John Booorman
Box Office	$46,1000,000
Awards	Faro Island Film Festival – Grand Jury Prize National Board of Reviewe, USA – Top Ten Films National Film Preservation Board, USA – National Film Registry

Main Cast	
Actor / Actress	**Screen Names**
Burt Reynolds	Lewis
Jon Voight	Ed
Ned Beatty	Bobby
Ronny Cox	Drew

Facts / More
Deliverance is referenced in the 2003 horror movie *Wrong Turn*.

1973

THE EXORCIST

Release Date	December 26, 1973
Budget	$12,000,000
Studio	Warner Bros., Hoya Productions
Run Time	121 minutes, varies depending on version
Sub-genre	Supernatural
Source / Inspiration	The Exorcist by William Peter Blatty (novel) 1971 Roland Doe: An alleged demonic possession of a 14-year-old boy in the 1940s. Some of the events reported were used as inspiration for Blatty's novel.
Writers	William Peter Blatty
Producers	William Peter Blatty
Directors	William Peter Friedkin
Box Office	$441,300,000
Awards	Academy Awards, USA – Best Writing, Screenplay Golden Globes, USA – Best Motion Picture (Drama) Golden Globes, USA – Best Supporting Actress (Linda Blair) Golden Globes, USA – Best Screenplay (William Peter Blatty) Golden Globes, USA – Best Director (William Friedkin) Academy of Science Fiction, Fantasy & Horror Films – Best Horror Film Academy of Science Fiction, Fantasy & Horror Films – Best Writer (William Peter Blatty) Academy of Science Fiction, Fantasy & Horror Films – Bet Make Up (Dick Smith) Academy of Science Fiction, Fantasy & Horror Films – Best Special Effects (Marcel Vercoutere) Empire Awards, UK – Movie Masterpiece Award Golden Screen, Germany – Golden Screen Award Motion Picture Sounds Editors, USA – Best Sound Editing (Sound Effects & Dialogue)

Main Cast

Actor / Actress	Screen Names
Linda Blair	Regan
Ellen Burstyn	Chris Macneil
Max von Sydow	Father Merrin
Jason Miller	Father Karras
Lee J. Cobb	Lt. William Kinderman

Facts / More

Adjusted for inflation, *The Exorcist* is the highest grossing R-Rated movie of all time.

Adjusted for inflation, *The Exorcist* is Warner Bros.' highest grossing movie of all time.

Upon release, the film was so disturbing that paramedics were called to multiple theaters from people fainting and acting hysterical.

While writing the original novel, William Peter Blatty was collecting unemployment benefits.

THE WICKERMAN

Release Date	December 6, 1973 - August 4, 1974 (depending on location)
Budget	£500,000
Studio	British Lion Films
Run Time	88 minutes
Sub-genre	Mystery Thriller
Source / Inspiration	---
Writers	Anthony Shaffer
Producers	Peter Snell, British Lion Films
Directors	Robin Hardy
Box Office	$58,341
Awards	Academy of Science Fiction, Fantasy & Horror Films, USA – Best Horror Film

Main Cast

Actor / Actress	Screen Names
Edward Woodward	Sergeant Howie
Christopher Lee	Lord Summerisle
Diane Cilento	Miss Rose
Britt Ekland	Willow

Facts / More

Christopher Lee agreed to appear in the film for free and considered this one of his greatest ever roles.

1974

THE TEXAS CHAINSAW MASSACRE

Release Date	October 11, 1974
Budget	$60,000 [increased to $140,000]
Studio	Bryanston Distributing Company
Run Time	83 minutes
Sub-genre	Slasher
Source / Inspiration	Murderer and Body Snatcher, Ed Gein (Edward Theodore Gein): The Butcher of Plainfield
Writers	Kim Henkel, Tobe Hooper
Producers	Vortex, Tobe Hooper
Directors	Tobe Hooper
Box Office	$30,900,000
Awards	Avoriaz Fantastic Film Festival – Critics Award

Main Cast	
Actor / Actress	**Screen Names**
Marilyn Burns	Sally
Allen Danziger	Jerry
Paul A. Partain	Franklin
Gunnar Hansen	Leatherface
William Vail	Kirk
Terri McMinn	Pam
John Dugan	Grandfather

Facts / More

You're able to drive by the original filming house in Texas and the owners are happy to allow visitors to take pictures from the road, but don't want people to approach their home.

The original budget was $60,000, but during the editing process they acquired another $80,000 in costs, forcing them to sell parts of their royalties.

TCM was banned in Finland for quarter of a century until the uncut version was finally released.

Ed Gein was some of the inspiration for the film, but Leatherface is not based on Ed Gein.

Despite being the Texas Chainsaw Massacre, only one character is killed by a chainsaw in the film.

In the ending scene, Gunnar Hansen was directed to "look frustrated" when Sally got away in the truck. Instead of stomping his feet he changed it to swinging the chainsaw in the air to scare Tobe Hooper as payback for unfair treatment of the cast during filming. Ironically, this decision turned into one of the most iconic scenes in horror history.

STRANGER IN THE HOUSE [BLACK CHRISTMAS]

Release Date	October 11, 1974 – December 20, 1974 (depending on location)
Budget	$620,000
Studio	Ambassador Film Distributors (Canada), Warner Bros., Canadian Film Development Corporation, Film Funding LTD.
Run Time	98 minutes
Sub-genre	Mystery-Thriller
Source / Inspiration	---
Writers	Roy Moore
Producers	Bob Clark, Canadian Film Development Corporation, Film Funding LTD.
Directors	Bob Clark
Box Office	$4,100,000
Awards	---

Main Cast	
Actor / Actress	**Screen Names**
Olivia Hussey	Jess
Keir Dullea	Peter
Margot Kidder	Barb

Facts / More
The entire film was shot over just 40 days.

YOUNG FRANKENSTEIN

Release Date	December 15, 1974
Budget	$2,780,000
Studio	20th Century Fox, Gruskoff Venture Films Crossbow Productions Inc.
Run Time	105 minutes – 106 minutes (depending on version)
Sub-genre	Comedy-Horror
Source / Inspiration	Frankenstein by Mary Shelley (novel), 1818
Writers	Gene Wilder, Mel Brooks
Producers	Michael Gruskoff, Gruskoff Venture Films Crossbow Productions Inc.
Directors	Mel Brooks
Box Office	$86,200,000
Awards	Academy of Science Fiction, Fantasy & Horror Films, USA – Best Horror Film
	Academy of Science Fiction, Fantasy & Horror Films, USA – Best Supporting Actor
	Academy of Science Fiction, Fantasy & Horror Films, USA – Best Director
	Academy of Science Fiction, Fantasy & Horror Films, USA – Best Make Up

	Academy of Science Fiction, Fantasy & Horror Films, USA – Best Set Decoration
	Golden Screens, Germany – Golden Screen
	Hugo Awards – Best Dramatic Presentation
	Science Fiction and Fantasy Writers of America – Best Dramatic Writing
	The Saturn Awards – Best Actor

Main Cast	
Actor / Actress	**Screen Names**
Gene Wilder	Dr. Frederick Frankenstein
Peter Boyle	The Monster
Marty Feldman	Igor
Madeline Kahn	Elizabeth
Kenneth Mars	Inspector Kemp
Terri Garr	Inga

Facts / More
Gene Wilder stated this was his favorite film he ever made.

1975

JAWS

Release Date	June 20, 1975
Budget	$9,000,000
Studio	Universal Studios
Run Time	124 minutes
Sub-genre	Thriller
Source / Inspiration	Jaws by Peter Benchley (novel), 1974
Writers	Peter Benchley, Carl Gottlieb
Producers	Richard D. Zanuck, David Brown, Zanuck/Brown Company, Universal Studios
Directors	Steven Spielberg
Box Office	$472,000,000
Awards	Academy Awards, USA – Best Sound
	Academy Awards, USA – Best Film Editing
	Academy Awards, USA – Best Music, Original Dramatic Score
	Golden Globes, USA – Best Original Score – Motion Picture
	Academy of Science Fiction, Fantasy & Horror Films, USA – Outstanding Film Award
	Golden Screen, Germany – Golden Screen Award
	Grammy Awards – Album of Best Original Score written for a Motion Picture or Television Special
	People's Choice Awards, USA – Favorite Motion Picture

Main Cast	
Actor / Actress	**Screen Names**
Roy Scheider	Chief Brody
Robert Shaw	Quint
Richard Dreyfuss	Hooper
Lorraine Gray	Ellen Brody
Murray Hamilton	Vaughn

Facts / More
Jaws became the first "summer blockbuster" when over 67 million Americans went to see it.
Steven Spielberg actually named the shark "Bruce" after his lawyer.
In the 2003 film *Finding Nemo*, the shark was named "Bruce" to pay tribute to the shark.

PROFONDO ROSSO [RED DEEP]

Release Date	March 7, 1975 – June 11, 1976 (depending on location)
Budget	---
Studio	Cineriz, Rizzoli Film, Seda Spettacoli
Run Time	126 minutes
Sub-genre	Mystery-Thriller
Source / Inspiration	---
Writers	Dario Argento, Benardino Zapponi
Producers	Salvatore Argento
Directors	Dario Argento
Box Office	$629,903
Awards	---

Main Cast	
Actor / Actress	**Screen Names**
David Hennings	Marcus Daly
Daria Nicolodi	Gianna Brezzi
Gabriele Lavia	Carlo

Facts / More
The story is set in Rome, but the majority of the film was shot in Turin, Italy.

SHIVERS

Release Date	September 26, 1975 – July 6, 1976 (depending on location)
Budget	$185,000
Studio	Cinepix Film Properties Inc., CFDC
Run Time	87 minutes
Sub-genre	Sci-FI
Source / Inspiration	---
Writers	David Cronenberg
Producers	Ivan Reitman
Directors	David Cronenberg
Box Office	$1,000,000 (Canadian)
Awards	Sitges Catalonian International Film Festival – Best Director

Main Cast	
Actor / Actress	**Screen Names**
Paul Hampton	Roger St. Luc
Joe Silver	Rollo Linsky

The original script was named *Invasion of the Blood Parasites*.

THE DAY OF THE LOCUST	
Release Date	May 7, 1975 – June 12, 1975 (UK) (depending on location)
Budget	---
Studio	Paramount Pictures
Run Time	144 minutes
Sub-genre	Thriller
Source / Inspiration	The Day of the Locust by Nathanael West (novel), 1939
Writers	Waldo Salt
Producers	Jerome Hellman
Directors	John Schlesinger
Box Office	---
Awards	BAFTA Awards – Best Costume Design National Board of Review – Top 10 Films Award

Main Cast	
Actor / Actress	**Screen Names**
Donald Sutherland	Homer
Karen Black	Faye
Burgess Meredith	Harry
Jackie Earl Haley	Adore
William Atherton	Tod

Facts / More
The original title of the source novel was *The Cheated*.

1976

CARRIE

Release Date	November 3, 1976 – November 16, 1796 (depending on location)
Budget	$1,800,000
Studio	United Artists
Run Time	98 minutes
Sub-genre	---
Source / Inspiration	*Carrie* by Stephen King (novel), 1974
Writers	Lawrence D. Cohen
Producers	Paul Monash
Directors	Brian De Palma
Box Office	$33,800,000 (North America)
Awards	Avoriaz Fantastic Film Festival – Grand Prize (director)
	National Society of Film Critics Awards – Best Actress

Main Cast	
Actor / Actress	**Screen Names**
Sissy Spacek	Carrie
Piper Laurie	Margaret White
John Travolta	Billy Nolan
Amy Irving	Sue Snell
William Katt	Tommy Ross

Facts / Moro
The film tips its hat to Normal Bates from Psycho (1960) with the high school being named "Bates High".
Carrie was the first Stephen King novel that was adapted into a film.

THE OMEN

Release Date	June 6, 1975 – June 25, 1976 (depending on location)
Budget	$2,800,000
Studio	20th Century Fox, Mace Neufeld Productions
Run Time	111 minutes
Sub-genre	Supernatural
Source / Inspiration	---
Writers	David Seltzer

Producers	Harvey Bernhard, Mace Neufeld Productions
Directors	Richard Donner
Box Office	$60,900,000 (North America)
Awards	Academy Awards, USA – Bet Music, Original Score
	British Society of Cinematographers – Best Cinematography
	Evening Standard British Film Awards – Best Actress

Main Cast	
Actor / Actress	**Screen Names**
Harvey Stephens	Damien
Gregory Peck	Robert Thorn
Lee Remick	Katherine Thorn
David Warner	Keith Jennings
Billie Whitelaw	Mrs. Baylock

Facts / More
Many writers refused to work on the project because of the subject matter.

LE LOCATAIRE [THE TENANT]

Release Date	May 26, 1976 – October 8, 1976 (depending on location)
Budget	---
Studio	Paramount Pictures
Run Time	126 minutes
Sub-genre	Thriller
Source / Inspiration	*The Tenant* by Roland Topor (novel, originally published in France), 1964
Writers	Gerard Brach, Roman Polanski
Producers	Andrew Braunsberg, Marianne Productions
Directors	Roland Polanski
Box Office	$5,100,000
Awards	---

Main Cast	
Actor / Actress	**Screen Names**
Roman Polanski	Trelkovsky
Isabelle adjani	Stella
Melvyn Douglas	Monsieur Zy

Facts / More
The film was shot in both English and French.

SQUIRM

Release Date	July 14, 1976 – July 30, 1976 (depending on location)
Budget	---
Studio	American International Pictures, The Squirm Company
Run Time	92 minutes
Sub-genre	---
Source / Inspiration	---
Writers	Jeff Lieberman
Producers	George Manasse
Directors	Jeff Lieberman
Box Office	---
Awards	---

Main Cast	
Actor / Actress	**Screen Names**
Don Scardino	Mick
Patricia Percy	Geri Sanders
R. A. Dow	Roger Grimes
Jean Sullivan	Naomi Sanders
Fran Higgins	Alma Sanders

Facts / More
Kim Basinger auditioned for the female lead of the film.

THE FOOD OF THE GODS

Release Date	June 18, 1976 – July 15, 1977 (depending on location)
Budget	---
Studio	American International Pictures
Run Time	88 minutes
Sub-genre	Sci-Fi
Source / Inspiration	The Food of the Gods and how it came to Earth by H. G. Wells (novel), 1904
Writers	Bert I. Gordon
Producers	Samuel Z. Arkoff, Bert I. Gordon
Directors	Bert I. Gordon
Box Office	$1,000,000
Awards	---

Main Cast	
Actor / Actress	**Screen Names**

Marjoe Gortner	Morgan
Pamela Franklin	Lorna
Ralph Meker	Bensington
John Cypher	Brian
Ida Lupinoo	Mrs. Skinner
John McLiam	Mr. Skinner
Belinda Balaski	Rita
Facts / More	
The film was nominated for Best Horror Film by The Academy of Science Fiction, Fantasy & Horror Films in 1976, but its average rating is 3.74/10.	

1977

THE HILLS HAVE EYES

Release Date	July 22, 1977
Budget	$350,000
Studio	Vanguard, Blood Relations Company
Run Time	89 minutes - 90 minutes (depending on version)
Sub-genre	Thriller
Source / Inspiration	---
Writers	Wes Craven
Producers	Peter Locke, Blood Relations Company
Directors	Wes Craven
Box Office	$25,000,000
Awards	Sitges – Catalonian International Film Festival

Main Cast	
Actor / Actress	**Screen Names**
Suze Lanier-Bramlett	Brenda Carter
Robert Houston	Bobby Carter
Martin Speer	Doug Wood
Dee Wallace	Lynne Wood
Russ Grieve	Big Bob Carter
Lance Gordon	Mars
John Steadman	Fred
James Whitworth	Jupiter
Virginia Vincent	Ethel Carter
Michaeel Berryman	Pluto
Janus Blythe	Ruby
Cordy Clark	Mama
Peter Locke	Mercury

Facts / More
Wees Craven once shared that the film was shot on cameras that were rented from a famous Californian pornographer.

THE EXORCIST II: THE HERETIC

Release Date	June 17, 1977
Budget	$14,000,000
Studio	Warner Bros.
Run Time	102 minutes – 117 minutes (depending on version)
Sub-genre	Supernatural
Source / Inspiration	Characters from the Exorcist (novel by William Peter Blatty)
Writers	William Goodhart
Producers	John Boorman, Richard Lederer
Directors	John Booman
Box Office	$30,700,000
Awards	---

Main Cast	
Actor / Actress	**Screen Names**
Linda Blair	Regan
Richard Burton	Father Philip Lamont
Louise Fletcher	Dr. Gene Tuskin
Max von Sydow	Father Merrin

Facts / More
This was the most expensive film Warner Bros. Had produced to date.
Linda Blair claimed that the film was one of the biggest disappointments of her career.

ERASERHEAD

Release Date	March 19, 1977 – Feb 3, 1978 (depending on location)
Budget	---
Studio	Libra Films, AFI Center for Advanced Studies
Run Time	89 minutes
Sub-genre	Fantasy
Source / Inspiration	---
Writers	David Lynch
Producers	David Lynch
Directors	David Lynch
Box Office	$7,000,000
Awards	Avoriaz Fantastic Film Awards – Antennae II Award

Main Cast	
Actor / Actress	**Screen Names**

Jack Nance	Henry Spencer
Charlotte Stewart	Mary X
Allen Joseph	Mr. X
Jeanne Bates	Mrs. X
Facts / More	
The script was only 22 pages long and there's no dialogue for the first 10 minutes as well as the last 25 minutes.	

HAUSU [HOUSE]

Release Date	July 30, 1977 (Japan) – September 1977 (depending on location)
Budget	---
Studio	Toho
Run Time	88 minutes
Sub-genre	Comedy-Horror
Source / Inspiration	Chigumi Obayashi (story)
Writers	Chico Katsura
Producers	Nobuhiko Obayashi, Toho
Directors	Nobuhiko Obayashi
Box Office	---
Awards	---

Main Cast	
Actor / Actress	**Screen Names**
Kimiko Ikegami	Oshare
Miki Jinbo	Kung Fu
Kumiko Ohba	Fantasy
Facts / More	
This film joined the Critereon Collection with spine #539.	

1978

HALLOWEEN

Release Date	October 25, 1978 – October 27, 1978 (depending on location)
Budget	$300,000
Studio	Compass International Pictures, Aquarius Releasing
Run Time	91 minutes
Sub-genre	Slasher, Thriller
Source / Inspiration	---
Writers	John Carpenter, Debra Hill
Producers	Debra Hill, Compass International Pictures, Falcon International Productions
Directors	John Carpenter
Box Office	$70,000,000
Awards	Avoriaz Fantastic Film Festival – Critics Award
	Los Angeles Film Critics Association Awards – New Generation Award

Main Cast	
Actor / Actress	**Screen Names**
Jamie Lee Curtis	Laurie
Donald Pleasance	Loomis
Tony Moran	Michael Myers (adult)
Will Sandin	Michael Myers (age 6)

Facts / More

John Carpenter also composed the score which has become one of the most iconic horror themes of all time.

The film was actually shot in the spring and that presented challenges such as procuring pumpkins. They also had to bring trash bags full of dead leaves to give the streets the appearance of fall.

The film's budget was increased from $300,000 to $325,000 to compensate Donald Pleasance for his five days of shooting, for which he was paid $25,000.

John Carpenter was only paid $10,000 to write, director and score the film.

DAWN OF THE DEAD

Release Date	September 1, 1978 – May 24, 1979 (depending on location)
Budget	$1,500,000
Studio	United Film Distribution Company, Laurel Group
Run Time	119 minutes – 127 minutes
Sub-genre	Adventure

Source / Inspiration	---
Writers	George A. Romero
Producers	Richard P. Rubinstein
Directors	George A. Romero
Box Office	$66,000,000
Awards	Golden Screen, Germany – Golden Screen Award

Main Cast	
Actor / Actress	**Screen Names**
David Emge	Stephen
Ken Foree	Peter
Scott H. Reiniger	Roger
Gaylen Ross	Francine

Facts / More
Some of the zombies in the film were actual amputees.

JAWS 2

Release Date	June 16, 1978
Budget	$30,000,000
Studio	Universal Studios, Zanuck/Brown Company
Run Time	116 minutes
Sub-genre	Thriller
Source / Inspiration	Peter Benchley's characters
Writers	Carl Gottlieb, Howard Sackler
Producers	Richard D. Zanuck, David Brown, Zanuck/Brown Company
Directors	Jeannot Szwarc
Box Office	$208,000,000
Awards	---

Main Cast	
Actor / Actress	**Screen Names**
Roy Scheider	Chief Brody
Lorraine Gray	Ellen Brody
Murray Hamilton	Mayor Vaughn
Jeffrey Kramer	Hendrix

Facts / More
This was the highest grossing sequel of its time until a year later when Rocky II overtook it.

PIRANHA

Release Date	August 3, 1978
Budget	$600,000
Studio	New World Pictures, United Artists, Piranha Productions
Run Time	94 minutes - 95 minutes (depending on location)
Sub-genre	Sci-Fi
Source / Inspiration	---
Writers	John Sayles, Richard Robinson
Producers	Jon Davison, Piranha Productions
Directors	Joe Dante
Box Office	$16,000,000
Awards	Academy of Science Fiction, Fantasy & Horror Films, USA – Saturn Awards

Main Cast	
Actor / Actress	**Screen Names**
Bradford Dillman	Paul Grogan
Belinda Balaski	Betsy

Facts / More
The film was said to be shot in just 30 days.
The fish were puppets on sticks.

INVASION OF THE BODY SNATCHERS

Release Date	December 22, 1978
Budget	$3,500,000
Studio	United Artists, Solofilm
Run Time	115 minutes
Sub-genre	Sci-Fi
Source / Inspiration	The Body Snatchers by Jack Finney (novel), 1955
Writers	W. D. Richter
Producers	Robert H. Solo
Directors	Philip Kaufman
Box Office	$24,900,000
Awards	Academy of Science Fiction, Fantasy & Horror Films, USA – Saturn Awards Avoriaz Fantastic Film Festival – Antennae II Award

Main Cast	
Actor / Actress	**Screen Names**
Donald Sutherland	Matthew Bennell

Brooke Adams	Elizabeth Discoll
Jeff Goldblum	Jack Bellicec
Veronica Cartwright	Nancy Bellicic
Facts / More	
Stephen King describes the decapitation scene in "Danse Macabre" and stated it was "absolutely brutal".	

DAY OF THE WOMAN [I SPIT ON YOUR GRAVE]

Release Date	November 22, 1978
Budget	$1,500,000
Studio	The Jerry Gross Organization, Cinemagic Pictures
Run Time	101 minutes
Sub-genre	Thriller
Source / Inspiration	---
Writers	Meir Zarchi
Producers	Joseph Zbeda
Directors	Meir Zarchi
Box Office	---
Awards	---
Main Cast	
Actor / Actress	**Screen Names**
Camille Keaton	Jennifer
Facts / More	

The film was originally titled "Day of the Woman" until it was renamed to its current title in 1980.

The main artwork with a woman in her underwear is actually Demi Moore.

DAMIEN: OMEN II

Release Date	June 9, 1978
Budget	$6,800,000
Studio	20th Century Fox, Mace Neufeld Productions
Run Time	107 minutes
Sub-genre	Supernatural
Source / Inspiration	Prequel, David Seltzer (characters)
Writers	Harvey Bernhard, Stanley Mann, Michael Hodges
Producers	Harvey Bernhard, Charles Orme, Mace Neufeld Productions
Directors	Don Taylor, Michael Hodges (uncredited)
Box Office	$26,500,000

| Awards | IFMCA, USA – FMCJ Award |
| | Motion Picture Sound Editors, USA – Golden Reel Award |

Main Cast	
Actor / Actress	**Screen Names**
Jonathan Scott-Taylor	Damien Thorn
Lee Grant	Ann Thorn
William Holden	Richard Thorn
Nicholas Pryor	Charles Warren

Facts / More
This is the only Omen movie that took place in the United States. Both *The Omen* and *The Final Conflict* took place in London.

1979

AMITYVILLE HORROR

Release Date	July 27, 1979
Budget	$4,700,000
Studio	American International Pictures, Cinema 77, Professional Films, Inc.
Run Time	118 minutes
Sub-genre	Supernatural
Source / Inspiration	The Amityville Horror by Jay Anson (novel based on true events), 1977 – Based on events reported by the Lutz family and investigated by Ed & Lorraine Warren.
Writers	Sandor Stern
Producers	Elliot Geisinger
Directors	Stuart Rosenberg
Box Office	$86,400,000
Awards	---

Main Cast	
Actor / Actress	**Screen Names**
James Brolin	George Lutz
Margot Kidder	Kathy Lutz
Rod Steiger	Father Delaney

Facts / More
James Brolin and Margot Kidder both visited the property where the supernatural events allegedly occurred, but neither of them believed the story despite Brolin becoming friends with the real George Lutz.

ALIEN

Release Date	May 25, 1979 – September 6, 1979 (depending on location)
Budget	$11,000,000
Studio	20th Century Fox, Brandywine Productions
Run Time	117 minutes
Sub-genre	Sci-Fi
Source / Inspiration	---
Writers	Dan O'Bannen, Ronald Shusett
Producers	Gordon Carroll, David Giler, Walter Hill, Brandywine Productions
Directors	Ridley Scott
Box Office	$106,300,00
Awards	Academy Awards, USA – Oscar

BAFTA Awards, USA – BAFTA Film Award	
Academy of Science Fiction, Fantasy & Horror Films, USA – Saturn Award	
Hugo Awards – Hugo Award	
San Sebastian International Film Festival – Silver Seashell	

Main Cast	
Actor / Actress	**Screen Names**
Sigourney Weaver	Ripley
Tom Skerritt	Dallas
Veronica Cartwright	Lambert
Harry Dean Stanton	Brett

Facts / More
Harrison Ford turned down the role of Dallas.
Ridley Scott did all the handheld camera work himself.
The original cut of the movie was over 3 hours long.

TOURIST TRAP

Release Date	March 14, 1979 – March 16, 1979 (depending on location)
Budget	$800,000
Studio	Compass International Pictures, Manson International Pictures, Mid-America Releasing, Charles Band Productions
Run Time	90 minutes
Sub-genre	---
Source / Inspiration	---
Writers	David Schmoeller, Larry Carroll
Producers	J. Larry Carroll, Charles Band Productions
Directors	David Schmoeller
Box Office	---
Awards	---

Main Cast	
Actor / Actress	**Screen Names**
Chuck Connors	Mr. Slausen
Jocelyn Jones	Molly
Tanya Roberts	Becky

Facts / More
The film was shot in just 24 days.

DRILLER KILLER

Release Date	June 15, 1979
Budget	---
Studio	Rochelle Films, Cult Epics
Run Time	96 minutes – 101 minutes (depending on version)
Sub-genre	Drama
Source / Inspiration	---
Writers	Nicolas St. John
Producers	Rochelle Weisberg, Rochelle Films
Directors	Abel Ferrera
Box Office	---
Awards	---

Main Cast	
Actor / Actress	**Screen Names**
Carolyn Mars	Carol Slaughter
Baybi Day	Pamela
Abel Ferrera	Reno Miller

Facts / More
This film was banned in the United Kingdom until 1999 and earned its Blu-ray release in 2016.

DRACULA

Release Date	July 13, 1979 – July 20, 1979
Budget	$12,200,000
Studio	Universal Pictures
Run Time	109 minutes
Sub-genre	Romance
Source / Inspiration	Dracula by Bram Stoker (novel), 1897 Dracula by Hamilton Deane (play), 1924
Writers	W. D. Richter
Producers	Marvin Mirisch, Walter Mirisch
Directors	John Badham
Box Office	$31,200,000
Awards	Academy of Science Fiction, Fantasy & Horror Films, USA – Saturn Award (Best Horror Film) IFMCA – IFMCA Award

Main Cast	
Actor / Actress	**Screen Names**

Frank Langella	Count Dracula
Laurence Olivier	Prof. Abraham Van Helsing
Donald Pleasence	Dr. Jack Seward
Jan Francis	Mina Van Helsing
Facts / More	
The film takes place in 1913.	

PHANTASM

Release Date	March 28, 1979
Budget	$300,000
Studio	AVCO Embassy Pictures
Run Time	89 minutes
Sub-genre	Sci-Fi
Source / Inspiration	---
Writers	Don Coscarelli
Producers	D. A. Coscarelli
Directors	Don Coscarelli
Box Office	$22,000,000
Awards	Academy of Science Fiction, Fantasy & Horror Films, USA – Saturn Award
	Avoriaz Fantastic Film Festival – Special Jury Award
Main Cast	
Actor / Actress	**Screen Names**
A. Michael Baldwin	Mike
Bill Thornbury	Jody
Reggie Bannister	Reggie
Kathy Lester	Lady in Lavender
Facts / More	
The film is called "Fantasmi" in Italy, which translates to "ghosts".	

NOSFERATU: PHANTOM DE NACHT [NOSFERATU THE VAMPYRE]

Release Date	January 17, 1979 – October 5, 1980 (depending on location)
Budget	$1,400,000
Studio	20th Century Fox, Werner Herzog, , Film Produktion, Gaumont, Zweites Deutsches Fernsehen
Run Time	107 minutes
Sub-genre	Drama

Source / Inspiration	Dracula by Bram Stoker (novel), 1897
	Nosferatu, eine Symphonie des Grauens by F. W. Murnau (silent horror film), 1922
Writers	Werner Herzog
Producers	Michael Gruskoff, Werner Herzog, Werner Herzog, , Film Produktion, Gaumont, Zweites Deutsches Fernsehen
Directors	Werner Herzog
Box Office	---
Awards	---

Main Cast	
Actor / Actress	**Screen Names**
Klaus Kinski	Count Dracula
Isabelle Adjani	Lucy Harker
Walter Ladengast	Dr. Van Helsing

Facts / More
Klais Kinski played Renfield in the 1970 *Count Dracula*.

WHEN A STRANGER CALLS

Release Date	September 28, 1979 – October 26, 1979 (depending on location)
Budget	$1,500,000
Studio	Colombia Pictures, Embassy Pictures, Melvin Simon Productions
Run Time	97 minutes
Sub-genre	Thriller
Source / Inspiration	---
Writers	Steve Feke, Fred Walton
Producers	Doug Chaplin, Steve Feke
Directors	Fred Walton
Box Office	$21,400,000
Awards	Avoriaz Fantastic Film Festival – Special Jury Award

Main Cast	
Actor / Actress	**Screen Names**
Carol Kane	Jill Johnson
Rutanya Alda	Mrs. Mandrakis
Carmen Argenziano	Dr. Mandrakis
Tony Beckley	Curt Duncan

Facts / More
Scream (1996) pays tribute to the film.

THE BROOD

Release Date	May 25, 1979 – June 1, 1979 (depending on location)
Budget	$1,400,000 (Canadian)
Studio	New World Pictures, Canadian Dilm Development Corporation
Run Time	92 minutes
Sub-genre	Sci-Fi
Source / Inspiration	---
Writers	David Cronenberg
Producers	Claude Heroux
Directors	David Cronenberg
Box Office	$5,000,000
Awards	Sitges – Catalonian International Film Festival – Prize of the International Critic' Jury (Special mention)

Main Cast	
Actor / Actress	**Screen Names**
Oliver Reed	Dr. Hal Raglan
Samantha Eggar	Nola Carveth
Art Hindle	Frank Carveth
Henry Beckman	Barton Kelly

Facts / More
This film is #777 in the Criterion Collection.

ARREBATO [RAPTURE]

Release Date	June 9, 1980 – August 26, 1983 (depending on location)
Budget	---
Studio	---
Run Time	105 minutes
Sub-genre	Fantasy
Source / Inspiration	---
Writers	Ivan Zulueta
Producers	Nicolas Astiarraga
Directors	Ivan Zulueta
Box Office	---
Awards	---

Main Cast	
Actor / Actress	**Screen Names**
Eusebio Poncela	Jose Sirgado

Cecilia Roth	Ana Turner
Will More	Pedro
Marta Fernandez Muro	Marta
Facts / More	
The first cut of the film was over three hour long.	

MOTEL HELL

Release Date	October 18, 1980 – October 24, 1980
Budget	$3,000,000
Studio	United Artists
Run Time	101 minutes
Sub-genre	Thriller
Source / Inspiration	---
Writers	Robert Jaffe, Steven-Charles Jaffe
Producers	Robert Jaffe, Steven-Charles Jaffe
Directors	Kevin Connor
Box Office	$6,300,000
Awards	---

Main Cast	
Actor / Actress	**Screen Names**
Rory Calhoun	Vincent Smith
Paul Linke	Bruce Smith
Nancy Parsons	Ida Smith
Nina Axelrod	Terry

Facts / More
The film was shot in five weeks.

THE SHINING

Release Date	May 23, 1980 – October 2, 1980
Budget	$19,000,000
Studio	Warner Bros., The Producer Circle Company, Peregrine Productions, Hawk Films
Run Time	119 minutes - 146 minutes (depending on version and release country)
Sub-genre	Drama
Source / Inspiration	The Shining by Stephen King (novel), 1977
Writers	Stanley Kubrick, Diane Johnson
Producers	Stanley Kubrick, The Producer Circle Company, Peregrine Productions, Hawk Films
Directors	Stanley Kubrick
Box Office	$47,000,000
Awards	Academy of Science Fiction, Fantasy & Horror Films, USA – Saturn Award

Main Cast	
Actor / Actress	**Screen Names**
Jack Nicholson	Jack Torrance
Shelley Duvall	Wendy Torrance
Danny Lloyd	Danny
Facts / More	
The iconic "Here's Johnny" scene took three days to film and around 60 doors were used.	

THE FOG

Release Date	February 1, 1980 – February 8, 1980
Budget	$1,100,000
Studio	AVCO Embassy Pictures, Debra Hill Productions
Run Time	90 minutes
Sub-genre	Thriller
Source / Inspiration	---
Writers	John Carpenter, Debra Hill
Producers	Debra Hill
Directors	John Carpenter
Box Office	$21,300,000
Awards	Avoriaz Fantastic Film Festival – Critics Award

Main Cast	
Actor / Actress	**Screen Names**
Adrienne Barbeau	Stevie Wayne
Jamie Lee Curtis	Elizabeth Solley
John Houseman	Mr. Machen
Tom Atkins	Nick Castle
Janet Leigh	Kathy Williams
Facts / More	
This was the first film where Jamie Lee Curtis and Janet Leigh, real-life mother and daughter, starred together.	

FRIDAY THE 13TH

Release Date	May 9, 1980
Budget	$550,000
Studio	Paramount Pictures, Warner Bros., Georgetown Productions Inc.
Run Time	95 minutes
Sub-genre	Mystery, Thriller

Source / Inspiration	---
Writers	Victor Miller
Producers	Sean S. Cunningham, Georgetown Productions Inc.
Directors	Sean S. Cunningham
Box Office	$59,800,000
Awards	---
Main Cast	
Actor / Actress	**Screen Names**
Betsy Palmer	Mrs. Vorhees
Kevin Bacon	Jack
Adrienne King	Alice
Jeannine Taylor	Marcie
Facts / More	

The film is mentioned in the opening sequence of Wes Craven's Scream when Ghostface asks Casey (Drew Barrymore) to name the killer in *Friday the 13th*.

CANNIBAL HOLOCAUST

Release Date	February 7, 1980
Budget	$100,000
Studio	United Artists, F.D. Cinematografica
Run Time	96 minutes
Sub-genre	Adventure
Source / Inspiration	---
Writers	Gianfranco Clerici, Georgio Stegani
Producers	Franco Di Nunzio, Franco Palaggi, F.D. Cinematografica
Directors	Ruggero Deodato
Box Office	---
Awards	
Main Cast	
Actor / Actress	**Screen Names**
Robert Kerman	Professor Harold Monroe
Francesca Ciardi	Faye Daniels
Perry Pirkanen	Jack Anders
Facts / More	

This was the second highest grossing film in Japan in 1983. Only second to Steven Spielberg's *E.T.*

PROM NIGHT

Release Date	July 18, 1980
Budget	$1,500,000
Studio	AVCO Embassy Pictures, Simcom Productions
Run Time	92 minutes
Sub-genre	Thriller
Source / Inspiration	---
Writers	William Gray, Robert Guza Jr.
Producers	Peter R. Simpson, Simcom Productions
Directors	Paul Lynch
Box Office	$14,800,000
Awards	---

Main Cast	
Actor / Actress	**Screen Names**
Leslie Nelson	Mr. Hammond
Jamie Lee Curtis	Kimberley Hammond
Casey Stevens	Nick McBride

Facts / More
This film is famous for being one of the only slashers with a sympathetic killer.

MOTHER'S DAY

Release Date	September 19, 1980
Budget	$115,000
Studio	United Film, Duty Productions, Saga Films A.B.
Run Time	91 minutes
Sub-genre	Comedy-Horror
Source / Inspiration	---
Writers	Charles Kaufman, Warren Leight
Producers	Michael Herz, Charles Kaufman, Duty Productions, Saga Films A.B.
Directors	Charles Kaufman
Box Office	---
Awards	---

Main Cast	
Actor / Actress	**Screen Names**
Nancy Hendrickson	Abbey
Deborah Luce	Jackie

Tiana Pierce	Trina
Facts / More	
Staying on budget, the film was shot for only $115,000.	

MANIAC

Release Date	January 30, 1981 - March 6, 1981
Budget	$350,000
Studio	Analysis Film Releasing Corporation, Magnum Motion Pictures Inc.
Run Time	88 minutes
Sub-genre	Slasher
Source / Inspiration	---
Writers	C.A. Rosenberg, Joe Spinell
Producers	Andrew W. Garroni, William Lustig, Magnum Motion Pictures Inc.
Directors	William Lustig
Box Office	$10,000,000
Awards	---

Main Cast	
Actor / Actress	**Screen Names**
Joe Spinell	Frank Zito
Caroline Munro	Anna D'Antoni
Facts / More	
This film was remade in 2012.	

PAURA NELLA CITTA DEI MORTI VIVENTI [CITY OF THE LIVING DEAD]

Release Date	August 11, 1980 – April 8, 1983
Budget	---
Studio	Medusa Distribuzoine, National Cinematografica, Dania Film
Run Time	93 minutes
Sub-genre	Supernatural
Source / Inspiration	---
Writers	Lucio Fulci, Dardano Saccetti
Producers	Mino Loy, Medusa Distribuzoine, National Cinematografica, Dania Film
Directors	Lucio Fulci
Box Office	$624,000 (approx)
Awards	---

Main Cast	

Actor / Actress	Screen Names
Christopher George	Peter Bell
Catriona MacColl	Mary Woodhouse
Facts / More	
Filmed in extremely hot temperatures. Some days reached 108 degrees fahrenheit.	

THE CHALENGING

Release Date	March 28,1980
Budget	$6,600,000
Studio	Pan-Canadian Film Distributors, Associated Film Distribution, Chessman Park Productions
Run Time	107 minutes
Sub-genre	---
Source / Inspiration	---
Writers	Russell Hunter, William Gray, Diana Maddox
Producers	Joel B. Michaels, Garth H. Drabinsky, Mario Kassar, Chessman Park Productions
Directors	Peter Medak
Box Office	$12,000,000
Awards	Fantafestival – Best Actor Genie Awards - Genie

Main Cast	
Actor / Actress	**Screen Names**
George C. Scott	John Russell
Trish Van Devere	Claire Norman
Facts / More	
The film's score was composed in London, England.	

1981

DAWN OF THE MUMMY

Release Date	December 11, 1981
Budget	$500,000
Studio	Harmony Gold USA, Goldfrab Distribution
Run Time	93 minutes
Sub-genre	---
Source / Inspiration	---
Writers	Daria Price, Ronald Dobrin, Frank Agrama
Producers	Frank Agrama
Directors	Frank Agrama
Box Office	---
Awards	---

Main Cast	
Actor / Actress	**Screen Names**
Brenda Siemer Scheider	Lisa
Barry Sattels	Bill

Facts / More

FRANKENSTEIN ISLAND

Release Date	November 27, 1981
Budget	---
Studio	---
Run Time	97 minutes
Sub-genre	Sci-Fi
Source / Inspiration	---
Writers	Jerry Warren
Producers	Robert Christopher, Jerry Warren
Directors	Jerry Warren
Box Office	---
Awards	---

Main Cast	
Actor / Actress	**Screen Names**

Robert Clarke	Dr. Paul Hadley
Steve Brodie	Jocko
Cameron Mitchell	Clay Jayson
Facts / More	
This was Jerry Warren's final film.	

GRADUATION DAY

Release Date	May 1, 1981 – May 8, 1981
Budget	$250,000
Studio	IFI/Scope III
Run Time	96 minutes
Sub-genre	Mystery
Source / Inspiration	---
Writers	Anne Marisse, Herb Freed, David Baughn
Producers	David Baughn, Herb Freed
Directors	Herb Freed
Box Office	$23,900,000
Awards	---

Main Cast	
Actor / Actress	**Screen Names**
Christopher George	Coach George Michaels
Patch MacKenzie	Nn Ramstead
E.J Peaker	Blondie
Facts / More	
The whole film was shot in under 21 days.	

THE PROWLER

Release Date	October 9, 1981
Budget	$1,000,000
Studio	Sandhurst
Run Time	89 minutes
Sub-genre	Thriller
Source / Inspiration	---
Writers	Glenn Leopold, Neal Barbera, Eric Lewald, Mark Edward Edens, Michael Edens, Sarah Higgins
Producers	Joseph Zito, David Streit

Directors	Joseph Zito
Box Office	< $1,000,000
Awards	---

Main Cast	
Actor / Actress	**Screen Names**
Vicky Dawson	Pam McDonald
Christopher Goutman	Mark London
Lawrence Tierney	Major Chatham
Joy Galaccum	Francis Rosemary Chatham

Facts / More
The film's international release title was "Rosemary's Killer".

WOLFEN

Release Date	July 24, 1981
Budget	$17,000,000
Studio	Orion Pictures, Warner Bros.
Run Time	115 minutes
Sub-genre	Supernatural
Source / Inspiration	The Wolfen (1978) Novel
Writers	David Eyre, Michael Wadleigh, Eric Roth
Producers	Rupert Hitzig, Orion Pictures
Directors	Michael Wadleigh
Box Office	$10,600,000
Awards	Avoriaz Fantastic Film Festival – Special Jury Award
	Motion Picture Sound Editors, USA – Golden Reel Award

Main Cast	
Actor / Actress	**Screen Names**
Albert Finney	Dewey Wilson
Diane Venora	Rebcca Neff
Edward James Olmos	Eddie Holt

Facts / More

SCANNERS

Release Date	January 14, 1981
Budget	$3,500,000

Studio	AVCO Embassy Pictures, Manson International
Run Time	103 minutes
Sub-genre	Science Fiction
Source / Inspiration	---
Writers	David Cronenberg
Producers	Claude Héroux
Directors	David Cronenberg
Box Office	$14,200,000
Awards	Academy of Science Fiction, Fantasy and Horror Films – Saturn Award Fantasporto – International Fantasy Film Award

Main Cast	
Actor / Actress	**Screen Names**
Jennifer O'Neill	Kim Obrist
Patrick McGoohan	Dr. Paul Ruth
Stephen Lack	Cameron Vale

Facts / More
This film is #712 in the Criterion Collection.

THE FUN HOUSE

Release Date	March 13, 1981
Budget	$300,000
Studio	Mace Neufeld Productions, Universal Pictures
Run Time	96 minutes
Sub-genre	---
Source / Inspiration	---
Writers	Lawrence J. Block
Producers	Stephen Bernhardt, Derek Power, Mace Neufeld, Mark L. Lester, Mace Neufeld Productions
Directors	Tobe Hooper
Box Office	$7,800,000
Awards	---

Main Cast	
Actor / Actress	**Screen Names**
Elizabeth Berridge	Amy Harper
Shawn Carson	Joey Harper
Jeanne Austin	Mrs. Harper
Jack McDermott	Mr. Harper

| Cooper Huckabee | Buzz Dawson |

Facts / More
The girls in the tent were local Miami strippers.
Tobe Hooper was bitten by a Brown Recluse spider during filming.

MY BLOOODY VALENTINE

Release Date	February 11, 1981
Budget	$2,300,000
Studio	Canadian Film Development Corporation, Secret Film Company, Paramount Pictures
Run Time	93 minutes
Sub-genre	Slasher
Source / Inspiration	---
Writers	Stephen Miller, John Beaird
Producers	John Dunning, Andre Link, Stephen Miller
Directors	George Mihalka
Box Office	$5,700,000
Awards	---

Main Cast	
Actor / Actress	**Screen Names**
Paul Kellman	T.J
Lori Hallier	Sara

Facts / More
Quentin Tarantino considers this his all-time favorite slasher film.

FRIDAY THE 13TH, PART II

Release Date	May 1, 1981
Budget	$1,250,000
Studio	Georgetown Production, Paramount Pictures
Run Time	87 minutes
Sub-genre	Slasher
Source / Inspiration	Sequel
Writers	Ron Kurz
Producers	Steve Miner
Directors	Steve Miner
Box Office	$21,7000,000
Awards	---

Main Cast	
Actor / Actress	**Screen Names**
Betsy Palmer	Mrs. Vorhees
Amy Steel	Ginny
John Furey	Paul
Warrington Gillette	Jason
Facts / More	
The original title of the movie was "Jason".	
Warrington plays the shortest version of Jason at 6'1.	

HALLOWEEN II

Release Date	October 30, 1981
Budget	$2,500,000
Studio	Dino De Laurentiis Corporation, Universal Pictures
Run Time	92 minutes
Sub-genre	Slasher
Source / Inspiration	---
Writers	John Carpenter, Debra Hill
Producers	John Carpenter, Debra Hill
Directors	Rick Rosenthal
Box Office	$25,500,000
Awards	Academy of Science Fiction, Fantasy & Horror Films – Saturn Award

Main Cast	
Actor / Actress	**Screen Names**
Jamie Lee Curtis	Laurie Strode
Donald Pleasence	Sam Loomis
Facts / More	
Every Halloween movie ends on Halloween night. This is the only movie to show the following morning.	

THE HOWLING

Release Date	March 13, 1981
Budget	$1,500,000
Studio	Embassy Pictures, International Film Investors, Wescom Productions
Run Time	91 minutes
Sub-genre	Supernatural

Source / Inspiration	The Howling (1977 novel) by Gary Brandner
Writers	John Sayles, Terence Winkless
Producers	Michael Finnell, Jack Conrad, International Film Investors, Wescom Productions
Directors	Joe Dante
Box Office	$17,900,000
Awards	Academy of Science Fiction, Fantasy & Horror Films – Saturn Award (Best Horror Film)
	Avoriaz Fantastic Film Festival – Critics Award

Main Cast	
Actor / Actress	**Screen Names**
Dee Wallace	Karen White
Patrick Macnee	Mr. George Waggner
Dennis Dugan	Chris

Facts / More
Tins of chili with the brand "Wolf" are seen throughout the movie.

AN AMERICAN WEREWOLF IN LONDON

Release Date	August 21, 1981
Budget	$5,800,000
Studio	Universal Pictures, Producers Sales Organization, Polygram Pictures, The Guber-Peters Company
Run Time	97 minutes
Sub-genre	Supernatural
Source / Inspiration	---
Writers	John Landis
Producers	George Folsey Jr.
Directors	John Landis
Box Office	$62,000,000
Awards	Academy Awards – Oscar (Best Makeup)
	Academy of Science Fiction, Fantasy & Horror Films – Saturn Award

Main Cast	
Actor / Actress	**Screen Names**
Jenny Agutter	Nurse Alex Price
David Naughton	David Kessler
Griffin Dunn	Jack Goodman

Facts / More
All the songs in the film have the word "moon" in their title.

THE EVIL DEAD

Release Date	October 15, 1981
Budget	$375,000
Studio	New Line Cinema, Renaissance Pictures
Run Time	85 minutes
Sub-genre	---
Source / Inspiration	---
Writers	Sam Raimi
Producers	Robert Tapert, Renaissance Pictures
Directors	Sam Raimi
Box Office	$2,400,000-$2,700,000
Awards	Academy of Science Fiction, Fantasy & Horror Films – Saturn Award (Best Low Budget Film) Sitges: Catalonian International Film Festival – Best Special Effects & Prize of the International Critics' Jury

Main Cast	
Actor / Actress	**Screen Names**
Bruce Campbell	Ashley Williams
Ellen Sandweiss	Cheryl

Facts / More
The Evil Dead was filmed in a real-life abandoned cabin.

1982

THE THING

Release Date	June 25, 1982
Budget	$15,000,000
Studio	The Turman-Foster Company, Universal Pictures
Run Time	109 minutes
Sub-genre	---
Source / Inspiration	Who Goes There? (novel) by John W. Campbell Jr.
Writers	Bill Lancaster
Producers	David Foster, Lawrence TurmanThe Turman-Foster Company
Directors	John Carpenter
Box Office	$19,600,000
Awards	---

Main Cast	
Actor / Actress	**Screen Names**
Kurt Russell	MacReady

Facts / More
It took Kurt Russell a year to grow the famous MacReady hair and beard.

POLTERGEIST

Release Date	June 4, 1982
Budget	$10,700,000
Studio	MGM, SLM Production Group, Mist Entertainment, Amblin Productions
Run Time	114 minutes
Sub-genre	Supernatural
Source / Inspiration	---
Writers	Steven Spielberg, Michael Grais, Mark Victor
Producers	Frank Marshall, Steven Spielberg
Directors	Tobe Hooper
Box Office	$121,700,000
Awards	BAFTA Awards – Best Special Visual Effects Academy of Science Fiction, Fantasy & Horror Films – Saturn Award (Best Horror Film, Best Supporting Actress and Best Make-Up)

Main Cast	
Actor / Actress	**Screen Names**
Heather O'Rourke	Carol Anne Freeling
Craig T. Nelson	Steve Freeling
JoBeth Williams	Diane Freeling
Facts / More	
Spielberg made the decision to hire Tobe Hooper after being impressed with his work on the Texas Chainsaw Massacre (1974)	

CREEPSHOW

Release Date	May 16, 1982 – November 10, 1982 (depending on location)
Budget	$8,000,000
Studio	Warner Bros., United Film Distribution Company, Lauren Show. Inc
Run Time	120 minutes
Sub-genre	---
Source / Inspiration	---
Writers	Stephen King
Producers	Richard P. Rubinstein
Directors	George A. Romero
Box Office	$21,000,000
Awards	---

Main Cast	
Actor / Actress	**Screen Names**
Leslie Nelson	Richard Vickers
Hal Holbrook	Henry Northrup
Adrienne Barbeau	Wilma Northhup
Facts / More	
This was the only George Romero film to open up as number one at weekend box office.	

HALLOWEEN 3: SEASON OF THE WITCH

Release Date	October 22, 1982
Budget	$2,500,000
Studio	Universal Pictures, Debra Hill Productions, Dino De Laurentiis Corporation
Run Time	98 minutes
Sub-genre	---
Source / Inspiration	---

Writers	Tommy Lee Wallace
Producers	Debra Hill. John Carpenter, Debra Hill Productions, Dino De Laurentiis Corporation
Directors	Tommy Lee Wallace
Box Office	$14,400,000
Awards	Academy of Science Fiction, Fantasy & Horror Films – Saturn Award (Best DVD/Blu-ray Collection 2015)

Main Cast	
Actor / Actress	**Screen Names**
Tom Atkins	Daniel Challis
Stacey Nelkin	Ellie Grimbridge

Facts / More
The gas station is also seen in John Carpenter's 1980 *The Fog*.

THE ENTITY

Release Date	September 30.1982
Budget	$9,000,000
Studio	20th Century Fox, American Cinema International
Run Time	125 minutes
Sub-genre	Supernatural
Source / Inspiration	The Entity by Frank De Felitta
Writers	Frank De Felitta
Producers	Harold Schneider, American Cinema International
Directors	Sidney J. Furie
Box Office	$13,300,000
Awards	Avoriaz Fantastic Film Festival – Best Actress

Main Cast	
Actor / Actress	**Screen Names**
Barbara Hershey	Carla Moran
Ron Silver	Phil Sneiderman
David Labiosa	Billy
George Coe	Dr. Webber
Margaret Blye	Indy Nash

Facts / More
The film's initial reviews were so bad that Barbara Hershey once thought that it was the worst decision of her career to take the role of Carla.

FRIDAY THE 13TH PART III

Release Date	August 13, 1982
Budget	$2,200,000
Studio	Paramount Pictures, Jason Inc.
Run Time	95 minutes
Sub-genre	Slasher
Source / Inspiration	Sequel
Writers	Martin Kitrosser, Carol Watson
Producers	Frank Mancuso Jr., Jason Inc.
Directors	Steve Miner
Box Office	$36,700,000
Awards	---

Main Cast	
Actor / Actress	**Screen Names**
Richard Brooker	Jason
Gloria Charles	Fox
David Katims	Chuck

Facts / More
The was the first film that used the iconic hockey mask and it has been in every sequel since.
This was Paramount's first 3-D film in over 25 years.

CHRISTINE

Release Date	December 9, 1983
Budget	$10,000,000
Studio	Colombia Pictures, Delphi Premier Productions, Polar Film
Run Time	110 minutes
Sub-genre	---
Source / Inspiration	Christine 9novel) by Stephen King
Writers	Bill Phillips
Producers	Richard Kobritz, Larry J. Franco, Delphi Premier Productions, Polar Film
Directors	John Carpenter
Box Office	$21, 000,000
Awards	---

Main Cast	
Actor / Actress	**Screen Names**
Keith Gordon	Arnie Cunningham
John Stockwell	Dennis Goulder
Alexaandra Paui	Leigh Cabot

Facts / More
15% of the entire budget went on cars and all but two were destroyed by the end of filming.

SLEEPAWAY CAMP

Release Date	November 18, 1983
Budget	$350,000
Studio	United Films Distribution Company, American Eagle Films
Run Time	84 minutes
Sub-genre	Slasher
Source / Inspiration	---
Writers	Robert Hiltzik
Producers	Jerry Silva, Michele Tatosian, American Eagle Films
Directors	Robert Hiltzik
Box Office	$1,000,000
Awards	---

Main Cast

Actor / Actress	Screen Names
Felissa Rose	Angela
Jonathan Tiersten	Ricky
Karen Fields	Judy
Christopher Collet	Paul
Facts / More	

CUJO	
Release Date	August 12, 1983
Budget	$8,000,000
Studio	Warner Bros., PSO International, Taft Entertainment, Sunn Classic Pictures
Run Time	93 minutes
Sub-genre	---
Source / Inspiration	Cujo (novel) by Stephen King
Writers	Don Carlos Dunaway, Barbara Turner
Producers	Robert Singer, Daniel H. Blatt, Taft Entertainment, Sunn Classic Pictures
Directors	Lewis Teague
Box Office	$21,200,000
Awards	Fantasporto – Audience Jury Award

Main Cast	
Actor / Actress	**Screen Names**
Dee Wallace	Donna Trenton
Danny Pintauro	Tad Trenton
Christopher Stone	Steve Kemp
Facts / More	

The origin of inspiration for Stephen King was his mechanic's intimidating dog that he met while getting his bike fixed.

Despite mixed reviews, Stephen King was fond of the adaptation. He also has a large influence on the script, but but declined taking any credit from Writer's Guild.

PSYCHO II	
Release Date	June 3, 1983
Budget	$5,000,000
Studio	Universal Pictures, Oak Industries
Run Time	113 minutes

Sub-genre	---
Source / Inspiration	Sequel
Writers	Tom Holland, Robert Bloch
Producers	Hilton A. Green, Bernard Schwartz, Universal Pictures, Oak Industries
Directors	Richard Franklin
Box Office	$34,700,000
Awards	---

Main Cast	
Actor / Actress	**Screen Names**
Anthony Perkins	Norman Bates
Vera Miles	Lila Crane Loomis
Meg Tilly	Mary

Facts / More
Quentin Tarantino stated this is one of his favorite films and he prefers it to the original 1960 Psycho.
The film was shot in a total of 32 days.

1984

A NIGHTMARE ON ELM STREET

Release Date	November 9, 1984
Budget	$1,100,000
Studio	New Line Cinema, Home Media Entertainment, Smart Egg Pictures
Run Time	91 minutes
Sub-genre	Slasher
Source / Inspiration	Cambodian Killing Fields Nightmares
Writers	Wes Craven
Producers	Robert Shaye
Directors	Wes Craven
Box Office	$57,000,000
Awards	Avoriaz Fantastic Film Festival - Critics Award
	Avoriaz Fantastic Film Festival - Special Mention

Main Cast

Actor / Actress	Screen Names
Heather Langenkamp	Nancy Thompson
Robert Englund	Freddy Krueger
John Saxon	Lt. Thompson
Ronee Blakley	Marge Thompson
Johnny Depp	Glen Lantz

Facts / More

Johnny Depp's first film.

"Elm Street" is not spoken in the film.

A boy, who's family escaped the Cambodian Killing Fields, was having nightmares of his past and this inspired the story. Another inspiration was a series of mysterious and unexplained nocturnal deaths that occurred in Asia with middle-aged men.

GREMLINS

Release Date	June 8, 1984
Budget	$11,000,000
Studio	Warner Bros., Amblin Entertainment
Run Time	106 minutes
Sub-genre	---

Source / Inspiration	Gremlin folklore
Writers	Chris Columbus
Producers	Michael Finnell
Directors	Joe Dante
Box Office	$212,900,000
Awards	Academy of Science-Fiction, Fantasy & Horror Films – Saturn Award
	Golden Screen, Germany – Golden Screen Award
	Young Artist Awards – Best Family Motion Picture

Main Cast	
Actor / Actress	**Screen Names**
Hoyt Axton	Randall Peltzer

Facts / More
Gremlins was released on the same day as Ghostbusters.
In the 2010's one of the Gremlins characters became a hit in the Mandela Effect community when people misremembered Stripe as Spike.

CHILDREN OF THE CORN

Release Date	March 9, 1984
Budget	$800,000
Studio	New World Pictures, Angeles Entertainment Group, Cinema Group, Hal Roach Studios. ,Inverness Productions, Plant Productions
Run Time	92 minutes
Sub-genre	---
Source / Inspiration	Children of the Corn (novel) by Stephen King
Writers	George Goldsmith
Producers	Donald P. Borchers, Terence Kirby, Angeles Entertainment Group, Cinema Group, Hal Roach Studios. ,Inverness Productions, Plant Productions
Directors	Fritz Kiersch
Box Office	$14,600,000
Awards	---

Main Cast	
Actor / Actress	**Screen Names**
Peter Horton	Burt
Linda Hamilton	Vicky
John Franklin	Isaac

Facts / More
The film spawned more sequels than any other Stephen King film.

NIGHT OF THE COMET

Release Date	November 16, 1984
Budget	$700,000
Studio	Atlantic Releasing Corporation, Thomas Colman and Michael Rosenblatt Productions, Film Development Fund
Run Time	95 minutes
Sub-genre	---
Source / Inspiration	---
Writers	Thom Eberhardt
Producers	Andrew Lane, Wayne Crawford
Directors	Thom Eberhardt
Box Office	$14,400,000
Awards	---

Main Cast	
Actor / Actress	**Screen Names**
Robert Beltran	Hector Gomez
Catherine May Stewart	Regina Belmont
Kelli Maroney	Samantha Belmont

Facts / More
The radio station was built in an abandoned warehouse.

THE TOXIC AVENGER

Release Date	April 11, 1986
Budget	$500,000
Studio	Troma Entertainment
Run Time	79 minutes
Sub-genre	---
Source / Inspiration	Lloyd Kaufman (story)
Writers	Joe Ritter
Producers	Michael Herz, Lloyd Kaufman, Stuart Strutin
Directors	Michael Herz, Llyod Kaufman
Box Office	$800,000
Awards	---

Main Cast	
Actor / Actress	**Screen Names**
Mitch Cohn	The Toxic Avenger
Andree Maranda	Sara

Jennifer Babtist	Wanda
Pat Ryan	Mayor Peter Belgoody
Facts / More	
The venue used for the Mexican restaurant is now a Popeye's Ruthreford, NJ.	

FRIDAY THE 13TH: THE FINAL CHAPTER

Release Date	April 13, 1984
Budget	$2,200,000
Studio	Paramount Pictures
Run Time	91 minutes
Sub-genre	Slasher
Source / Inspiration	Sequel
Writers	Barney Cohen, Bruce Hidemi Sakow (story),
Producers	Frank Mancuso Jr., Paramount Pictures
Directors	Joseph Zito
Box Office	$33,000,000
Awards	---
Main Cast	
Actor / Actress	**Screen Names**
Corey Feldman	Tommy
Erich Anderson	Rob
Judie Aronson	Samantha
Facts / More	
The movie's release date was Friday the 13th.	

JAYWHEELERMOVIES.COM

1985

FRIGHT NIGHT

Release Date	August 2, 1985
Budget	$9,250,000
Studio	Colombia Pictures, Vistar Films
Run Time	106 minutes
Sub-genre	Supernatural
Source / Inspiration	---
Writers	Tom Holland
Producers	Herb Jaffe, Vistar Films
Directors	Tom Holland
Box Office	$24,900,000
Awards	Academy of Science Fiction, Fantasy & Horror Films – Saturn Award
	Avoriaz Fantastic Film Festival – Dario Argento Award
	Fantasporto – Critic's Award

Main Cast	
Actor / Actress	**Screen Names**
Chris Sarandon	Jerry Dandridge
William Ragsdale	Charley Brewster
Amanda Bearse	Amy Peterson
Roddy McDowell	Peter Vincent

Facts / More
Fright Night was the first vampire film to spend over a million dollars on special effects.

A NIGHTMARE ON ELM STREET 2: FREDDY'S REVENGE

Release Date	November 1, 1985
Budget	$3,000,000
Studio	New Line Cinema, Heron Communications, Smart Egg Pictures
Run Time	87 minutes
Sub-genre	Slasher
Source / Inspiration	Sequel
Writers	David Chaskin, Wes Craven
Producers	Robert Shaye

Directors	Jack Sholder
Box Office	$30,000,000
Awards	---

Main Cast	
Actor / Actress	**Screen Names**
Robert Englund	Freddy Krueger
Mark Patton	Jesse Walsh
Kim Myers	Lisa Webber

Facts / More
The is the only Nightmare on Elm Street film where the lead character is male.
Robert Englund has stated that this was his least favorite film of the franchise.

LIFE FORCE

Release Date	June 21, 1985
Budget	$25,000,000
Studio	TriStar Pictures
Run Time	101 minutes – 116 minutes (depending on version)
Sub-genre	---
Source / Inspiration	The Space Vampires (novel) by Colin Wilson
Writers	Dan O'Bannen, Don Jakoby
Producers	Yoram Globus, Menahem Golan, Cannon Films
Directors	Tobe Hooper
Box Office	$11,600,000
Awards	Sitges Catalonian International Film Festival – Caixa de Catalunya (effects)

Main Cast	
Actor / Actress	**Screen Names**
Steve Railsback	Col. Tom Carlson
Peter Firth	Col. Colin Caine
Frank Finlay	Dr. Hans Fallada

Facts / More
The model for the space ship was an artichoke.

DAY OF THE DEAD

Release Date	July 19, 1985
Budget	$4,000,000
Studio	United Film Distribution Company, Laurel Entertainment

Run Time	100 minutes
Sub-genre	---
Source / Inspiration	---
Writers	George A. Romero
Producers	Richard P. Rubinstein, Laurel Entertainment
Directors	George A. Romero
Box Office	$34,000,000
Awards	Academy of Science Fiction, Fantasy & Horror Films – Saturn Award
	Sitges Catalonian International Film Festival – Caizaa de Catalunya (best actress)

Main Cast	
Actor / Actress	**Screen Names**
Lori Cardille	Sarah
Terry Alexander	John

Facts / More
Real pig intestines were used during the gore scenes.

RETURN OF THE LIVING DEAD

Release Date	August 16, 1985
Budget	$4,000,000
Studio	Orion Pictures, Hemdale, Cinema '84
Run Time	91 minutes
Sub-genre	---
Source / Inspiration	---
Writers	Dan O'Bannen, Rudy Ricci (story), John A. Russo (story), Russell Streiner (story)
Producers	Tom Fox, Graham Henderson, Cinema '84, Hemdale
Directors	Dan O'Bannen
Box Office	$14,200,000
Awards	---

Main Cast	
Actor / Actress	**Screen Names**
Clu Gulager	Burt
James Karen	Frank
Don Calfer	Ernie

Facts / More
The nuclear cannon at the end of the film was actually a World War II German Howitzer.

RE-ANIMATOR

Release Date	October 18, 1985
Budget	$2,000,000
Studio	Empire International Pictures, Re-Animator Productions
Run Time	86 minutes
Sub-genre	---
Source / Inspiration	Herbert West-Reanimator (short story) by H. P. Lovecraft
Writers	Dennis Paoli, William Norris, Stuart Gordon
Producers	Brian Yuzna, Re-Animator Productions
Directors	Stuart Gordon
Box Office	$2,000,000
Awards	Avoriaz Fantastic Film Festival – Special Mention
	Fantafestival – Best Film & Best Special Effects
	Sitges Catalonian International Film Festival – Caixa De Catalunya

Main Cast	
Actor / Actress	**Screen Names**
Jeffrey Combs	Herbert West
Bruce Abbott	Dan Cain
Barbara Crampton	Megan Halsey
David Gale	Dr. Carl Hill

Facts / More
The entire film was shot in only 18 days.

SILVER BULLET

Release Date	October 11, 1985
Budget	$7,000,000
Studio	Paramount Pictures
Run Time	95 minutes
Sub-genre	Supernatural
Source / Inspiration	Cycle of the werewolf (novel) by Stephen King
Writers	Stephen King
Producers	Agostino Dino De Laurentiis, Martha De Laurentiis
Directors	Dan Attias
Box Office	$12,400,000
Awards	---

Main Cast

Actor / Actress	Screen Names
Gary Busey	Uncle Red
Corey Haim	Marty Colsaw
Facts / More	
This is the tenth Stephen King film adaptation.	

CAT'S EYE

Release Date	April 12, 1985
Budget	$7,000,000
Studio	MGM, De Laurentiis Entertainment Group
Run Time	94 minutes
Sub-genre	---
Source / Inspiration	Quitters Inc. and The Ledge (short stories) by Stephen King
Writers	Stephen King
Producers	Agostino Dino De Laurentiis, Martha Schumacher
Directors	Lewis Teague
Box Office	$13,100,000
Awards	---

Main Cast	
Actor / Actress	**Screen Names**
Drew Barrymore	Amanda
James Woods	Dick Morrison
Alan King	Dr. Vinny Donnati
Facts / More	
This was the first Stephen King film to receive a PG-13 rating.	

FRIDAY THE 13TH: A NEW BEGINNING

Release Date	March 22, 1985
Budget	$2,200,000
Studio	Paramount Pictures, Georgetown Productions Terror Inc.
Run Time	92 minutes
Sub-genre	Slasher
Source / Inspiration	Sequel
Writers	Martin Kitrosser, David Cohen, Danny Steinmann
Producers	Timothy Silver, Georgetown Productions Terror Inc.
Directors	Danny Steinmann

Box Office	$22,000,000
Awards	---

Main Cast	
Actor / Actress	**Screen Names**
Tom Morga (uncredited)	Jason
Johnny Hock (uncredited)	Jason [opening scene]
Dominick Brascia	Joey
Todd Bryant	Neil

Facts / More
This was the last film directed by Danny Steinmann.

THE FLY

Release Date	August 15, 1986
Budget	$15,000,000
Studio	20th Century Fox, Brooksfilms, SLM Production Group
Run Time	96 minutes
Sub-genre	Sci-Fi
Source / Inspiration	The Fly (short story) by George Langeelaan
Writers	Charles Edward Pogue, David Cronenberg
Producers	Stuart Cornfeld
Directors	David Cronenberg
Box Office	$60,600,000
Awards	Academy Awads – Oscar (best makeup)
	Academy of Science Fiction, Fantasy & Horror Films – Saturn Award
	Avoriaz Fantastic Film Festival – Special Jury Award
	Canadian Society of Cinematography Award – CSC Award
	National Board of Review – NBR Winner

Main Cast	
Actor / Actress	**Screen Names**
Jeff Goldblum	Seth Brundle
Geena Davis	Veroniva Quaife

Facts / More
Jeff Goldblum's makeup took 5 hours to apply the most extensive parts.

POLTERGEIST II: THE OTHER SIDE

Release Date	May 23, 1986
Budget	$19,000,000
Studio	MGM
Run Time	91 minutes
Sub-genre	Supernatural
Source / Inspiration	Sequel
Writers	Mark Victor, Michael Grais
Producers	Mark Victor, Michael Grasi, MGM

Directors	Brian Gibson
Box Office	$41,000,000
Awards	BMI Film & TV Awards - BMI

Main Cast	
Actor / Actress	**Screen Names**
JoBeth Williams	Diane Freeling
Craig T. Nelson	Steve Freeling
Heather O'Rourke	Carol Anne Freeling

Facts / More
Heather O'Rourke said the film was boring and not scary after its release.

ALIENS

Release Date	July 18, 1986
Budget	$18,500,000
Studio	20th Century Fox, Brandywine Productions
Run Time	137 minutes
Sub-genre	Science Fiction
Source / Inspiration	---
Writers	James Cameron, David Giler, Walter Hill
Producers	Brandywine Productions, Gale Anne Heard
Directors	James Cameron
Box Office	$183,000,000
Awards	Academy Awards USA – Oscar (Best Effects)
	BAFTA Awards – BAFTA Best Special Visual Effects)
	Academy of Science Fiction, Fantasy & Horror Films – Saturn Award
	ASCAP Film and Television Music Awards – ASCAP Award (Top Box Office Films)
	Hugo Awards – Hugo Award (Best Dramatic Presentation)
	Kinema Junpo Awards – Reader's Choice Award
	Motion PictureSounds Editors, USA - Best Sound Editing

Main Cast	
Actor / Actress	**Screen Names**
Sigourney Weaver	Ripleey
Carrie Henn	Newt
Paul Reiseer	Burke
Michael Biehn	Corporal Hicks
Lance Henrikson	Bishop

Facts / More
This was Carie Henn's only acting role. She became a teacher.
Ripley's miniatur bathroom in her apartment is actually a British Airways toilet purchased from the airline.

THE TEXAS CHAINSAW MASSACRE II

Release Date	August 22, 1986
Budget	$4,500,000
Studio	Cannon Releasing, The Cannon Group, Inc.
Run Time	101 minutes
Sub-genre	Slasher
Source / Inspiration	Sequel
Writers	L. M. Kit Carson, Tobe Hooper
Producers	Menahem Golan, Yoram Globus, The Cannon Group, Inc.
Directors	Tobe Hooper
Box Office	$8,000,000
Awards	---

Main Cast	
Actor / Actress	**Screen Names**
Dennis Hopper	Lieutenant 'Lefty' Enright
Caroline Williams	Vanita 'Stretch' Brock
Jim Seidow	Cook

Facts / More
Tobe Hooper owns the chainsaw from the film and keeps it in a glass display case.

CRITTERS

Release Date	April 11, 1986
Budget	$3,000,000
Studio	New Lin Cinema, Sho Films
Run Time	85 minutes
Sub-genre	---
Source / Inspiration	---
Writers	Dominic Muir, Stephen Herek
Producers	Rupert Harvey, Sho Films
Directors	Stephen Herek
Box Office	$13,200,000
Awards	---

Main Cast

Actor / Actress	Screen Names
Dee Wallace	Helen Brown
M. Emmet Walsh	Harv
Billy Green Bush	Jay Brown
Facts / More	
This was Stephn Herek's directorial debut.	

FRIDAY THE 13TH PART VI: JASON LIVES

Release Date	August 1, 1986
Budget	$3,000,000
Studio	Paramount Pictures, Terror Inc.
Run Time	86 minutes
Sub-genre	Slasher
Source / Inspiration	Sequel
Writers	Tom McLoughlin
Producers	Don Behrns, Terror Inc.
Directors	Tom McLoughlin
Box Office	$19,400,000
Awards	---

Main Cast	
Actor / Actress	**Screen Names**
C. J. Graham	Jason
Thom Matthews	Tommy
Jennifer Cooke	Megan
Darcy DeMoss	Nikki
Facts / More	
The film as shot in 40 days.	
Jennifer Cooke retired from her acting career after appearing in the film.	

MANHUNTER

Release Date	August 15, 1986
Budget	$15,000,000
Studio	De Laurentiis Entertainment Group, Red Dragon Productions
Run Time	120 minutes
Sub-genre	---
Source / Inspiration	Red Dragon (novel) by Thomas Harris

Writers	Michael Mann
Producers	Richard A. Roth, De Laurentiis Entertainment Group, Red Dragon Productions
Directors	Michael Mann
Box Office	$8,600,000
Awards	Cognac Festival du Film Policier – Critics Award

Main Cast	
Actor / Actress	**Screen Names**
William Peterson	Will Graham
Kim Greist	Molly Graham
Joan Allen	Reba McClane
Brian Cox	Dr. Hannibal Lecter

Facts / More
The prison where Hannibal is being held is the High Museum of Art in Atlanta, Georgia.

1987

HELLRAISER

Release Date	September 10, 1987
Budget	$1,000,000
Studio	Entertainment Film Distributors, Film Futures
Run Time	93 minutes
Sub-genre	---
Source / Inspiration	The Hellbound Heart (novel) by CliveBarker
Writers	Clive Barker
Producers	Christopher Figg, Film Futures
Directors	Clive Barker
Box Office	$14,6000,000
Awards	Avoriaz Fantastic Film Festival – Fear Section Award
	Fantasporto – Critic's Award

Main Cast

Actor / Actress	Screen Names
Doug Bradley	Lead Cenobite
Andrew Robinson	Larry
Claire Higgins	Julia

Facts / More

It took 6 hours to apply Doug Bradley's make-up.

CREEPSHOW II

Release Date	May 1, 1987
Budget	$3,500,000
Studio	New World Pictures, Laurel Entertainment
Run Time	92 minutes
Sub-genre	---
Source / Inspiration	Sequel
Writers	George A. Romero
Producers	David Ball, Laurel Entertainment
Directors	Michael Gornick
Box Office	$14,000,000

Awards	---

Main Cast	
Actor / Actress	**Screen Names**
---	---

Facts / More
Arnold Schwarzenegger was said to be considered for a role in the film.

A NIGHTMARE ON ELM STREET 3: DREAM WARRIORS

Release Date	February 27, 1987
Budget	$4,600,000
Studio	New Line Cinema, Herron Communications, Smart Egg Pictures
Run Time	96 minutes
Sub-genre	Slasher
Source / Inspiration	Sequel
Writers	Wes Craven, Bruce Wagner, Frank Darabont, Chuck Russell
Producers	Robert Shaye, New Line Cinema, Herron Communications, Smart Egg Pictures
Directors	Chuck Russell
Box Office	$44,800,000
Awards	Fantasporto – Critic's Award

Main Cast	
Actor / Actress	**Screen Names**
Heather Langenkamp	Nancy Thompson
Craig Wasson	Neil Gordon
Robert Englund	Freddy Krueger
Patricia Arquette	Kristen Parker

Facts / More
This is the first film where Robert Englund's character is called "Freddy Krueger" instead of "Fred".
The original UK poster of the Freddy Snake eating a woman was withdrawn and replaced.
This is considered by many fans as the best film in the franchise.

EVIL DEAD II

Release Date	March 13, 1987
Budget	$3,500,000
Studio	Rosebud Releasing Corporation, Renaissance Pictures
Run Time	84 minutes

Sub-genre	---
Source / Inspiration	Sequel
Writers	Sam Raimi, Scott Spiegel
Producers	Robert Tapert, Renaissance Pictures
Directors	Sam Raimi
Box Office	$10,900,000
Awards	---

Main Cast	
Actor / Actress	**Screen Names**
Bruce Campbell	Ashley Williams
Sarah Berry	Annie Knowby
Dan Hicks	Jake

Facts / More
Thee eyeball swallow shot was filmed in reverse.

THE LOST BOYS

Release Date	July 31, 1987
Budget	$8,500,000
Studio	Warner Bros.
Run Time	98 minutes
Sub-genre	Supernatural
Source / Inspiration	---
Writers	Jan Fischer, James Jeremias, Jeffrey Boam
Producers	Harvey Bernhard
Directors	Joel Schumacher
Box Office	$32,200,000
Awards	---

Main Cast	
Actor / Actress	**Screen Names**
Corey Haim	Sam
Jason Patric	Michael
Diane West	Lucy

Facts / More
The film was shot in just 3 weeks.

1988

93

CHILD'S PLAY

Release Date	November 9, 1988
Budget	$9,000,000
Studio	MGM, U.A Communications Co., United Artists
Run Time	87 minutes
Sub-genre	Slasher
Source / Inspiration	---
Writers	Don Mancini, John Lafia, Tom Holland
Producers	David Kirschner, United Artists
Directors	Tom Holland
Box Office	$44,200,000
Awards	Academy of Science Fiction, Fantasy & Horror Films – Saturn Award

Main Cast

Actor / Actress	Screen Names
Catherine Hicks	Karen Barclay
Chris Sarandon	Mike Norris
Alex Vincent	Andy Barclay

Facts / More

The original working title of the film was "Batteries not Included" until it was discovered that Steven Spielberg was making a film with the same title. The film title then changed to "Blood Buddy" before settling with "Child's Play".

THE BLOB

Release Date	August 5, 1988
Budget	$10,000,000
Studio	TriStar Pictures, Palisades California, Inc.
Run Time	95 minutes
Sub-genre	Science Fiction
Source / Inspiration	The Blob (1958) movie
Writers	Chuck Russell, Frank Darabont
Producers	Jack H. Harris, Elliot Kastner
Directors	Chuck Russell
Box Office	$8,200,000

| Awards | Avoriaz Fantastic Film Festival – Best Special Effects |

Main Cast	
Actor / Actress	**Screen Names**
Kevin Dillon	Brian Flagg
Shawnee Smith	Meg Penny
Candy Clark	Fran Hewitt

Facts / More
The was release 30 years after the original, but had over 80 times the budget.

KILLER CLOWNS FROM OUTER SPACE

Release Date	May 27, 1988
Budget	$1,800,000
Studio	Trans World Entertainment, Chiodo Bros.
Run Time	88 minutes
Sub-genre	---
Source / Inspiration	---
Writers	Charles Chiodo, Stephen Chiodo
Producers	Charles Chiodo, Stephen Chiodo, Edward Chiodo, Chiodo Bros.
Directors	Stephen Chiodo
Box Office	$43,625,000
Awards	---

Main Cast	
Actor / Actress	**Screen Names**
Grant Cramer	Mike Tobacco
Suzanne Snyder	Debbie Stone
John Allen Nelson	Dave Hansen

Facts / More
In a deleted scene, one of the klowns got beaten up

NIGHT OF THE DEMONS

Release Date	October 14, 1988
Budget	$1,200,000
Studio	International Film Marketing, Paragon Arts International, Halloween Partners Ltd., Meridian Pictures
Run Time	89 minutes
Sub-genre	---

Source / Inspiration	---
Writers	Joe Augustyn
Producers	Joe Augustyn, Paragon Arts International, Halloween Partners Ltd., Meridian Picutres
Directors	Kevin S. Tenney
Box Office	$3,100,000
Awards	---

Main Cast	
Actor / Actress	**Screen Names**
Hal Havins	Stooge
Alvin Alexis	Rodger
Allison Barron	Helen

Facts / More
The film was shot in just four weeks.

A NIGHTMARE ON ELM STREET 4: THE DREAM MASTER

Release Date	August 19, 1988
Budget	$6,500,000
Studio	New Line Cinema, Heron Communications, Smart Egg Pictures
Run Time	93 minutes
Sub-genre	Slasher
Source / Inspiration	Sequel
Writers	Brian Helgeland, Jim Wheat, Ken Wheat
Producers	Robert Shaye, Rachel Talalay, New Line Cinema, Heron Communications, Smart Egg Pictures
Directors	Renny Harlin
Box Office	$49,400,000
Awards	Sitges – Catalonian International Film Festival – Best Special Efffects Young Artists Award – Young Artist Award

Main Cast	
Actor / Actress	**Screen Names**
Robert Englund	Freddy Krueger
Rodney Eastman	Joey
Duane Davis	Jock

Facts / More
The success of this film convinced producers to create Freddy's Nightmare, the TV series, in 1988.

THEY LIVE

Release Date	November 4, 1988
Budget	$3,000,000
Studio	Universal Pictures, Carolco Pictures, Alive Firms, Larry Franco Productions
Run Time	94 minutes
Sub-genre	---
Source / Inspiration	Eight O'Clock in the Morning (short story) by Ray Nelson
Writers	John Carpenter
Producers	Larry Franco
Directors	John Carpenter
Box Office	$13,000,000
Awards	---

Main Cast	
Actor / Actress	**Screen Names**
Roddy Piper	Nada
Keith David	Frank
Meg Foster	Holly
Peter Jason	Gilbert

Facts / More
Roddy Piper, who was married at the time, refused to take his wedding ring off during filming and you can see him wearing it in a few scenes.

HALLOWEEN 4: THE RETURN OF MICHAEL MYERS

Release Date	October 21, 1988
Budget	$5,000,000
Studio	Galaxy International Releasing, Trancas International
Run Time	88 minutes
Sub-genre	Slasher
Source / Inspiration	Sequel
Writers	Alan B. McElroy
Producers	Paul Freeman
Directors	Dwight H. Little
Box Office	$17,800,000
Awards	---

Main Cast	
Actor / Actress	**Screen Names**
George P. Wilbur	Michael Myers

Donald Pleasance	Dr. Sam Loomis
Ellie Cornell	Rachel Carruthers
Danielle Harris	Jamie Lloyd
Facts / More	
Danielle Harris sold the clown costume to a fan.	
Similarly to the original Halloween movie, leaves had to be imported and squash painted to look like pumpkins.	

FRIDAY THE 13TH PART VII: THE NEW BLOOD

Release Date	May 13, 1988
Budget	$2,800,000
Studio	Paramount Pictures
Run Time	88 minutes
Sub-genre	Slasher
Source / Inspiration	Sequel
Writers	Daryl Haney, Manuel Fidello
Producers	Iain Paterson
Directors	John Carl Buechler
Box Office	$19,100,000
Awards	---
Main Cast	
Actor / Actress	**Screen Names**
Kane Hodder	Jason
Facts / More	
Jason appeared unmasked for more time in this film than any other.	

POLTERGEIST III

Release Date	June 10, 1988
Budget	$9,500,000
Studio	MGM
Run Time	98 minutes
Sub-genre	Supernatural
Source / Inspiration	Sequel
Writers	Gary Sherman, Brian Taggert
Producers	Barry Bernadi, MGM
Directors	Gary Sherman
Box Office	$14,100,000

Awards	---

Main Cast	
Actor / Actress	**Screen Names**
Heather O'Rourke	Carol Anne
Tom Skerritt	Bruce Gardner
Nancy Allen	Patricia Gardner

Facts / More
Heather O'Rourke looked bloated throughout the film after being prescribed incorrect medicine that caused her body and face to swell.

PET SEMATARY

Release Date	April 21, 1989
Budget	$11,500,000
Studio	Paramount Pictures
Run Time	103 minutes
Sub-genre	---
Source / Inspiration	Pet Sematary (novel) by Stephen King
Writers	Stephen King
Producers	Richard P. Rubenstein, Paramount Pictures
Directors	Mary Lambert
Box Office	$57,500,000
Awards	Avoriaz Fantastic Film Festival – Audience Award

Main Cast	
Actor / Actress	**Screen Names**
Dale Midkiff	Louis Creed
Denise Crosby	Rachel Creed
Fred Gwynne	Jud Crandall

Facts / More
Stephen King was on set for most of the shooting. The shooting location was just 20 minutes from his home in Maine.
George A. Romero was was originally set to direct, but the filming was delayed and Mary Lambert took the position.

HALLOWEEN 5: THE REVENGE OF MICHAEL MYERS

Release Date	October 13, 1989
Budget	$5,000,000
Studio	Galaxy Releasing, Magnum Pictures, Trancas International
Run Time	97 minutes
Sub-genre	Slasher
Source / Inspiration	Sequel
Writers	Michael Jacbos, Dominique Othenin-Girard, Shem Bitterman
Producers	Ramsey Thomas, Magnum Pictures, Trancas International
Directors	Dominique Othenin-Girard

Box Office	$11,600,000
Awards	---
Main Cast	
Actor / Actress	**Screen Names**
Don Shanks	Michael Myers
Donald Pleasance	Dr. Sam Loomis
Ellie Cornell	Rachel
Facts / More	

This was the only Halloween film to never be released in Italy.

This was the lowest grossing film in the series.

SANTA SANGRE

Release Date	May 19, 1989 – May 30, 1990 (depending on location)
Budget	$787,000
Studio	Mainline Pictures, Expanded Entertainment
Run Time	123 minutes
Sub-genre	---
Source / Inspiration	---
Writers	Alejandro Jodorowsky, Roberto Leoni, Claudio Argento
Producers	Claudio Argento
Directors	Alejandro Jodorowsky
Box Office	Unknown
Awards	Academy of Science Fiction, Fantasy & Horror Films – Saturn Award
Main Cast	
Actor / Actress	**Screen Names**
Axel Jodorowsky	Fenix
Blanca Guerra	Concha
Guy Stockwell	Orgo
Sabrina Dennison	Alma
Thelma Tixou	Tattoed Woman
Adan Jodorowsky	Young Fenix
Facts / More	

As a tribute to Mexican horror films, Santa Sangre includes a scene with masked wrestlers and a superwoman named La Santa.

This film is included in Empire's 500 Greatest Movies of All Time.

A NIGHTMARE ON ELM STREET 5: THE DREAM CHILD

Release Date	August 11, 1989
Budget	$8,000,000
Studio	New Line Cinema, Heron Communications, Smart Egg Pictures
Run Time	90 minutes
Sub-genre	Slasher
Source / Inspiration	Sequel
Writers	John Skipp, Craig Spector, Leslie Bohem
Producers	Robert Shaye, Rupert Harvey, New Line Cinema, Heron Communications, Smart Egg Pictures
Directors	Stephen Hopkins
Box Office	$22,100,000
Awards	---

Main Cast	
Actor / Actress	**Screen Names**
Robert Englund	Freddy Krueger
Lisa Wilcox	Alice
Kelly Jo Minter	Yvonne
Erika Anderson	Greta

Facts / More
Stephen King and Frank Miller were were offered the job of writing and directing the movie.
The film open at number #3 at the box office, but became the lowest grossing film in the franchise.

FRIDAY THE 13TH PART VIII: JASON TAKES MANHATTAN

Release Date	July 28, 1989
Budget	$5,500,000
Studio	Paramount Pictures
Run Time	100 minutes
Sub-genre	Slasher
Source / Inspiration	Sequel
Writers	Rob Hedden
Producers	Randy Cheveldave
Directors	Rob Hedden
Box Office	$14,300,000
Awards	---

Main Cast	
Actor / Actress	**Screen Names**

Kane Hodder	Jason
Tim Mirkovich	Young Jason
Tiffany Paulsen	Suzi
Todd Caldecott	Jim
Facts / More	

This is the longest Friday the 13th film at 100 minute run time.

At the time, this was the lowest grossing film in the series and prompted Paramount Pictures to sell the series to New Line Cinema.

1990

NIGHTBREED	
Release Date	February 16, 1990
Budget	$11,000,000
Studio	20th Century Fox, Morgan Creek Productions
Run Time	102 minutes
Sub-genre	---
Source / Inspiration	Cabel (novel) by Clive Barker
Writers	Clive Barker
Producers	Gabriella Martinelli, John Turtle, Joe Roth, Morgan Creek Productions
Directors	Clive Barker
Box Office	$16,000,000
Awards	Amsterdam Fantastic Film Festival – Silver Scream Awards
	Avoriaz Fantastic Film Festival – Special Jury Award
	Fantasporto – Critic's Award

Main Cast	
Actor / Actress	**Screen Names**
Craig Sheffer	Aaron / Cabal
Anne Bobby	Lori Winston
David Cronberg	Dr. Phillip K Decker

Facts / More

CHILD'S PLAY II	
Release Date	November 9, 1990
Budget	$13,000,000
Studio	Universal Pictures, Living Doll Productions
Run Time	84 minutes
Sub-genre	Slasher
Source / Inspiration	Sequel
Writers	Don Mancini
Producers	David Kirschner
Directors	John Lafia

Box Office	$35,800,000
Awards	---

Main Cast	
Actor / Actress	**Screen Names**
Brad Dourif	Chucky (voice)
Alex Vincent	Andy Barclay
Jenny Agutter	Joanne Simpson
Gerrett Graham	Phil Simpson

Facts / More
The original script had an opening court room scene dealing with the events of the previous film, but it was cut before filming. Elements of the scene were featured in a similar court room scene in Curse of Chucky (2013).

LEATHERFACE: THE TEXAS CHAINSAW MASSACRE III

Release Date	January 12, 1990
Budget	$2,000,000
Studio	New Line Cinema
Run Time	85 minutes
Sub-genre	Slasher
Source / Inspiration	Sequel
Writers	David J. Schow
Producers	Robert Engelman
Directors	Jeff Burr
Box Office	$5,700,000
Awards	---

Main Cast	
Actor / Actress	**Screen Names**
R. A. Mihailoff	Leatherface
Kate Hodge	Michelle
Ken Foree	Benny
William Butler	Ryan

Facts / More
The film's trailer was completed before production began and before they even had a director.
The only TCM not to be filmed in Texas. It was filmed outside Los Angeles, California. The farm house and gas station was a set that was built.
The chainsaw in the movie weighed approximately 80 lbs.

THE EXORCIST III

Release Date	August 17, 1990
Budget	$11,000,000
Studio	20th Century Fox, Morgan Creek Productions
Run Time	110 minutes
Sub-genre	Supernatural
Source / Inspiration	Sequel
Writers	William Peter Blatty
Producers	Carter DeHaven, James G. Robinson, Morgan Creek Productions
Directors	William Peter Blatty
Box Office	$44,000,000
Awards	Academy of Science Fiction, Fantasy & Horror Films – Saturn Award

Main Cast	
Actor / Actress	**Screen Names**
George C. Scott	Kinderman
Ed Flanders	Father Dyer
Brad Dourif	The Gemini Killer
Jason Miller	Patient X

Facts / More
The Gemini Killer was based on the real-life Zodiac Killer. There was also a film based on the events (Zodiac 2007)

1991

FREDDY'S DEAD: THE FINAL NIGHTMARE

Release Date	September 13, 1991
Budget	$11,000,000
Studio	New Line Cinema
Run Time	89 minutes
Sub-genre	Slasher
Source / Inspiration	Sequel
Writers	Michael De Luca
Producers	Robert Shaye, Aron Warner, New Line Cinema
Directors	Rachel Talalay
Box Office	$34,900,000
Awards	---

Main Cast	
Actor / Actress	**Screen Names**
Robert Englund	Freddy Krueger
Lisa Zane	Maggie Burroughs
Lezlie Deane	Tracy

Facts / More
Peter Jackson was originally hired to write the screenplay. He wrote a draft, but it was never used. His screenplay saw Freddy aging and getting weaker in the dreamworld and then the teens of Springwood would throw drug-fueled slumber parties where the teens would enter the dream world and beat Freddy up.

THE SILENCE OF THE LAMBS

Release Date	February 14, 1991
Budget	$19,000,000
Studio	Orion Pictures, Strong Heart Productions
Run Time	118 minutes
Sub-genre	Psychological Thriller
Source / Inspiration	The Silence of the Lambs (novel) by Thomas Harris
Writers	Ted Tally
Producers	Kenneth Utt, Edward Saxon, Ron Bozzman, Strong Heart Productions
Directors	Jonathan Demme
Box Office	$272,700,000

Awards	Academy Awards, USA – Oscar
	BAFTA Awards – BAFTA Film Award
	Academy of Science Fiction, Fantasy & Horror Films – Saturn Award
	Amsterdam Fantastic Film Festival – Silver Scream Award
	ASCAP Film & Television Music Awards – ASCAP Award
	ASECAN – ASECAN Awards
	Awards Circuit Community Awards – ACCA
	Berlin International Film Festival – Silver Berlin Bear Award
	Blue Ribbon Awards – Blue Ribbon Award
	Boston Society of Film Critic's Award – BSFC Award
	Chicago Film Critic's Association Awards – CFCA Award
	Dallas-Fort Worth Film Critics Association Awards – DFWFCA Award
	Director's Guild of America, USA – DGA Award
	Edgar Allan Poe Awards – Edgar (Best Motion Picture)
	Fangoria Chainsaw Awards – Chainsaw Award
	Golden Globes, USA – Golden Globe
	Golden Screen, Germany – Golden Screen
	Hochi Film Awards – Hochi Film Award
	Jupiter Awards – Jupiter Award
	Kansas City Film Critics Circle Awards – KCFCC Award
	National Board of Review, USA – NBR Award
	National Film Preservation Board, USA – Naational Film Registry Award
	New York Film Critics Circle Award – NYFCC Award
	People's Choice Awards – People's Choice Award
	PGA Awards – PGA Award
	Sant Jordi Awards – Sant Jordi Award
	Writer's Guild of America, USA – WGA Award

Main Cast	
Actor / Actress	**Screen Names**
Jodie Foster	Clarice Starling
Sir. Anthony Hopkins	Dr. Hannibal Lecter
Ted Levine	Jame Gumb (Buffalo Bill)
Scott Glenn	Jack Crawford
Lawrence T. Wrentz	Agent Burroughs
Kasi Lemmons	Ardelia Mapp

This film has the highest box office in this Almanac thus far.

During Clarice and Hannibal's first meet on screen, Anthony Hopkins improvised and mocked her Southern accent to which Jodie Foster felt personally attacked. She later thanks Anthony for the impromptu mocking as it gave her a genuine terrified reaction which was kept in the scene.

The FBI fully cooperated with the production as they saw it as a good marketing tool to recruit more female FBI agents.

The Silence of the Lambs recouped its budget within the first week of release.

One of the filming techniques during the Hannibal Clarice interactions was to zoom out on Clarice and zoom in on Hannibal which gives the character of Hannibal a more terrifying presence.

CAPE FEAR

Release Date	November 15, 1991
Budget	$35,000,000
Studio	Universal Pictures, Amblin Entertainment, Cappa Films, Tribeca Productions
Run Time	128 minutes
Sub-genre	---
Source / Inspiration	Cape Fear (1962), The Executioners (novel) by John D. MacDonald
Writers	Wesley Strick
Producers	Barbara De Fina, Amblin Entertainment, Cappa Films, Tribeca Productions
Directors	Martin Scorsese
Box Office	$182,300,000
Awards	Awards Circuit Community Awards – ACCA
	BMI Film & Television Awards – BMI Film Music Award
	Chicago Film Critic's Association Awards – CFCA Award
	Jupiter Awards – Jupiter Award
	Kansas City Film Critics Circle Awards – KCFCC Award

Main Cast

Actor / Actress	Screen Names
Robert De Niro	Max Cady
Jessica Lange	Leigh Bowden
Juliette Lewis	Danielle Bowden
Nick Nolte	Sam Bowden

Facts / More

It took over a year to convince Martin Scorsese to direct the film.

Drew Barrymore failed her audition for the role of Danielle Bowden and called it "the biggest disaster of my life".

THE PEOPLE UNDER THE STAIRS

Release Date	November 1, 1991
Budget	$6,000,000
Studio	Universal Pictures, Alive Films
Run Time	102 minutes
Sub-genre	---
Source / Inspiration	---
Writers	Wes Craven
Producers	Stuart M. Besser, Marianne Maddalena Alive Films
Directors	Wes Craven
Box Office	$31,4000,000
Awards	Avoriaz Fantastic Film Festival – Special Jury Award
	Brussel's International Festival of Fantasy Film – Pegasus Audience Award

Main Cast	
Actor / Actress	**Screen Names**
Brandon Quintin Adams	Fool
Everett McGill	Man
Wendy Robie	Woman
Bill Cobbs	Grandpa Booker
Ving Rhames	Leroy

Facts / More
The film earned its total $6M budget within a few days of its theatrical release.

CHILD'S PLAY 3

Release Date	August 30, 1991
Budget	$13,000,000
Studio	Universal Pictures
Run Time	90 minutes
Sub-genre	Slasher
Source / Inspiration	Sequel
Writers	Don Mancini
Producers	Robert Latham Brown
Directors	Jack Bender
Box Office	$20,500,000
Awards	Academy of Science Fiction, Fantasy & Horror Films, USA – Saturn Award

Main Cast

Actor / Actress	Screen Names
Brad Dourif	Chucky (voice)
Justin Whalin	Andy Barclay
Perrey Reeves	De Silva
Travis Fine	Shelton
Facts / More	

Don Mancini was put under pressure from Universal Pictures and was asked to begin the screenplay for the third installment before the second film had even released. This was his least favorite as he was out of ideas after the second film.

This film was released just 9 months after Child's Play II.

This is Brad Dourif's least favorite movie in the series.

CANDYMAN

Release Date	October 6, 1992
Budget	$9,000,000
Studio	TriStar Pictures, Propaganda Films, Polygram Filmed Entertainment
Run Time	101 minutes
Sub-genre	Supernatural
Source / Inspiration	The Forbidden (Books of Blood) by Clive Barker
Writers	Bernard Rose
Producers	Steve Golin, Sigurjon Sighvatsson, Alan Poul, Propaganda Films, Polygram Filmed Entertainment
Directors	Bernard Rose
Box Office	$25,800,000
Awards	Academy of Science Fiction, Fantasy & Horror Films, USA – Saturn Award
	Avoriaz Fantastic Film Festival – Audience Award, Best Actress, Best Music
	Fangoria Chainsaw Awards – Chainsaw Award

Main Cast

Actor / Actress	Screen Names
Tony Todd	Candyman / Daniel Robitaille
Virginia Madsen	Helen Lyle
Xander Berkeley	Trevor Lyle
Kasi Lemmons	Bernie

Facts / More

Tony Todd admitted he was stung by bees 26 times during the Candyman trilogy.

Tony Todd negotiated a $1,000 bonus for every time he was stung by a bee. He was stung 23 times during the first film, earning him a $23,000 bonus.

Eddie Murphy was considered for the role of Candyman, but at 5'9 he was too short so they went with Tony Todd who is 6'5.

BRAM STOKER'S DRACULA

Release Date	November 13, 1992
Budget	$40,000,000
Studio	Colombia Pictures, American Zoetrope, Osiris Films
Run Time	128 minutes

Sub-genre	Supernatural
Source / Inspiration	Dracula (1897 novel) by Bram Stoker
Writers	James V. Hart
Producers	Francis Ford Coppola, Fred Fuchs, Charles Mulvehill, American Zoetrope, Osiris Films
Directors	Francis Ford Coppola
Box Office	$215,800,000
Awards	Academy Awards, USA – Oscar
	20/20 Awards – Felix Award
	Academy of Science Fiction, Fantasy & Horror – Saturn Award
	ASCAP Film & Television Music Awards – ASCAP Award
	Awards Circuit Community Awards – ACCA
	Chicago Film Critics Association Awards – CFCA Award
	Fangoria Chainsaw Awards – Chainsaw Award
	Fotogramas de Plata - Fotogramas de Plata
	International Monitor Awards – Monitor Award
	Jupiter Awards – Jupiter Award

Main Cast

Actor / Actress	Screen Names
Gary Oldman	Dracula
Winona Ryder	Mina Murray / Elisabeta
Anthony Hopkins	Professor Abraham Van Helsing
Keanu Reeves	Jonathan Harker
Richard E. Grant	Dr. Jack Seward
Sadie Frost	Lucy Westrnra

Facts / More

Francis Ford Coppola came up with the idea that the laws of physics could be bend when in the presence of a supernatural being, such as a vampire. This is why shadows act independently from the figure or object casting it, why cat can walk on the ceilings and why liquid can drip upwards.

SLEEPWALKERS

Release Date	April 10, 1992
Budget	$15,000,000
Studio	Colombia Pictures, Ion Pictures, Victor & Grais Productions
Run Time	91 minutes
Sub-genre	---
Source / Inspiration	---
Writers	Stephen King

Producers	Michael Grais, Mark Victor, Dimitri Logothetis, Nabeel Zahid, Ion Pictures, Victor & Grais Productions
Directors	Mick Garris
Box Office	$30,500,000
Awards	Fangoria Chainsaw Awards – Chainsaw Award
	Fantafestival – Best Actress, Best Direction, Best Film, Best Screenplay

Main Cast	
Actor / Actress	**Screen Names**
Ron Pearlman	Captain Soames
Brian Krause	Charles Brady
Madchen Amick	Tanya Robertson
Alice Krige	Mary Brady

Facts / More
This is the only film that has Stephen King and Clive Barker in the same scene.

THE LAWNMOWER MAN

Release Date	March 6, 1992
Budget	$10,000,000
Studio	New Line Cinema, Allied Vision, Fuji Eight Company Ltd., Lane Pringle Productions, Angel Studios
Run Time	108 minutes, 142 minutes (Director's Cut)
Sub-genre	---
Source / Inspiration	The Lawnmower Man (short story) by Stephen King
Writers	Brett Leonard, Gimel Everett
Producers	Gimel Everett, Milton Subotsky, Masayo Takiyama, Allied Vision, Fuji Eight Company Ltd., Lane Pringle Productions, Angel Studios
Directors	Brett Leonard
Box Office	$32,100,000
Awards	---

Main Cast	
Actor / Actress	**Screen Names**
Jeff Fahey	Jobe Smith
Pierce Brosnan	Dr. Lawrence Angelo
Jenny Wright	Marnie Burke

Facts / More
The eight minutes of computer generated effect took 7 people a total of 8 months to complete with a budget of $500,000.

ARMY OF DARKNESS

Release Date	October 9, 1992 – February 19, 1993 (depending on location)
Budget	$11,000,000
Studio	Universal Pictures, Dino De Laurentiis Communications, Renaissance Pictures, Introvision International
Run Time	81 minutes, 88 minutes (international cut)
Sub-genre	---
Source / Inspiration	---
Writers	Sam Raimi, Ivan Raimi
Producers	Robert Tapert, Dino De Laurentiis Communications, Renaissance Pictures, Introvision International
Directors	Sam Raimi
Box Office	$21,500,000
Awards	Academy of Science Fiction, Fantasy & Horror Films, USA – Saturn Award Brussels International Festival of Fantasy Films – Golden Raven Award Fangoria Chainsaw Awards – Chainsaw Award Fantasporto – Critics' Award

Main Cast

Actor / Actress	Screen Names
Bruce Campbell	Ash
Embeth Davidtz	Shiela
Marcus Gilbert	Lord Arthur
Ian Abercrombie	Wiseman

Facts / More

In the original draft, Ash lost an eye.

Released in Japan as "Captain Supermarket".

S-Mart is a chain of grocery stores in Mexico.

BODY BAGS	
Release Date	August 8, 1993
Budget	Unknown
Studio	187 Corp., Showtime Networks
Run Time	91 minutes
Sub-genre	---
Source / Inspiration	---
Writers	Billy Brown, Dan Angel
Producers	Dan Angel, Sandy King, 87 Corp., Showtime Networks
Directors	John Carpenter
Box Office	---
Awards	---

Main Cast	
Actor / Actress	**Screen Names**
John Carpenter	The Coroner
Tom Arnold	Morgue Worker
Tobe Hooper	Morgue Worker
Sam Raimi	Dead Bill
Peter Jason	Gent

Facts / More
John Carpenter spent 3 hours in the make up chair for his role of the Coroner.
Was made as a pilot episode for a proposed anthology, but Showtime ultimately decided against it.

LEPRECHAUN	
Release Date	January 8, 1993
Budget	$1,000,000
Studio	TriMark Pictures
Run Time	92 minutes
Sub-genre	---
Source / Inspiration	---
Writers	Mark Jones
Producers	Jeffrey B. Mallian

Directors	Mark Jones
Box Office	$8,600,000
Awards	Fangoria Chainsaw Awards – Chainsaw Awards

Main Cast	
Actor / Actress	**Screen Names**
Warwick Davis	Leprechaun
Jennifer Anniston	Tory
Mark Holton	Ozzie

Facts / More

This was Jennifer Anniston's film debut.

This was also the first film for TriMark Pictures.

JASON GOES TO HELL: THE FINAL FRIDAY

Release Date	August 13, 1993
Budget	$3,000,000
Studio	New Line Cinema, Sean S. Cummingham Films
Run Time	88 minutes, 90 minutes (Unrated cut)
Sub-genre	Slasher
Source / Inspiration	Sequel
Writers	Dean Lorey, Jay Huguely
Producers	Sean S. Cunningham, Debbie Hayn-Cass, Sean S. Cummingham Films
Directors	Adam Marcus
Box Office	$15,900,000
Awards	---

Main Cast	
Actor / Actress	**Screen Names**
Kane Hodder	Jason
Kari Keegan	Jessica Kimble
John D. LeMay	Steven Freeman
Steven Williams	Creighton Duke

Facts / More

Jason's heart was also used as Monkey Man's heart in Dusk Till Dawn (1996).

The reason the title is "Jason Goes To Hell: The Final Friday" is because New Line Cinema didn't have the rights to Friday the 13th.

Friday the 13th being unlucky is thought to stem from the bible when Judas, who betrayed Jesus, was the 13th guest to sit down at the last supper.

1994

NEW NIGHTMARE	
Release Date	October 14, 1994
Budget	$8,000,000
Studio	New Line Cinema
Run Time	12 minutes
Sub-genre	Slasher
Source / Inspiration	Sequel
Writers	Wes Craven
Producers	Marianne Madalena
Directors	Wes Craven
Box Office	$19,800,000
Awards	Fangoria Chainsaw Awards – Chainsaw Award
	Fantasporto – International Fantasy Film Award

Main Cast	
Actor / Actress	**Screen Names**
Heather Langenkamp	Nancy Thompson
Robert Englund	Freddy Krueger
Miko Hughes	Dylan
Matt Winston	Chuck
Wes Craven	Wes Craven

Facts / More

The final Freddy Krueger film until the iconic character went up against the Crystal Lake killer in Freddy vs Jason (2003).

In real life, Heather Langenkamp had a stalker and Wes Craven got her permission to weave it into the story.

Robert Englund has said this is his favorite film of the franchise. This may be because Freddy Krueger is much closer to Wes Craven's initial ideas for the character where he is less comical and more menacing.

INTERVIEW WITH THE VAMPIRE	
Release Date	November 11, 1994
Budget	$60,000,000
Studio	Warner Bros., The Geffen Film Company
Run Time	122 minutes
Sub-genre	Supernatural

Source / Inspiration	Interview the with Vampire (novel) by Anne Rice
Writers	Anne Rice
Producers	David Geffen, Stephen Woolley, The Geffen Film Company
Directors	Neil Jordan
Box Office	$223,700,000
Awards	BAFTA Awards – BAFTA Film Award
	Academy of Science Fiction, Fantasy & Horror Films, USA – Saturn Award
	ASCAP Film & Television Music Awards – ASCAP Award
	Awards Circuit Community Awards – ACCA, Honorable Mentions
	Blockbuster Entertainment Awards – Blockbuster Entertainment Award
	Boston Society of Film Critics Award – BSFC Award
	British Society of British Cinematographers – Best Cinematography Award
	Chicago Film Critics Association Award – CFCA Award
	Fangoria Chainsaw Awards – Chainsaw Award
	International Horror Guild – IGH Award
	Italian National Syndicate of Film Journalists – Silver Ribbon Award
	MTV Movie & TV Awards – MTV Movie Award
	Razzie Awards – Razzie Award
	Sci-Fi Universe Magazine – Universe Reader's Choice Award
	Young Stars Awards – Young Stars Award

Main Cast

Actor / Actress	Screen Names
Brad Pitt	Louis
Tom Cruise	Lestat
Christian Slater	Malloy
Thandiwe Newton	Yvette
Kirsten Dunst	Claudia

Facts / More

All the actors plating vampires were required to hang upside down for up to 30 minutes at a time so the blood would rush to their heads in order for the make up artists to trace the bulging veins.

The original choice for the character of Malloy was River Phoenix, but when he died Christian Slater was given the role. Slater donated his entire salary from the film to Phoenix's favorite charities.

This was the first film production to be given permission to close two lanes of traffic on the Golden Gate Bridge in San Francisco.

Natalie Portman auditioned for the role of Claudia, but it went to Kirsten Dunst.

MARY SHELLEY'S FRANKENSTEIN

Release Date	November 4, 1994
Budget	$45,000,000
Studio	TriStar Pictures, Japan Satellite Broadcasting, Inc., The Indyprod Company, American Zoetrope
Run Time	123 minutes
Sub-genre	Supernatural
Source / Inspiration	Frankenstein (novel) by Mary Shelley
Writers	Steph Lady, Frank Darabont
Producers	Francis Ford Coppola, James V. Hart, John Veitch, Japan Satellite Broadcasting, Inc., The Indyprod Company, American Zoetrope
Directors	Kenneth Branagh
Box Office	$112,000,000
Awards	---

Main Cast	
Actor / Actress	**Screen Names**
Robert De Niro	Creature
Kenneth Branagh	Victor
Helena Bonham Carter	Elizabeth

Facts / More
Tim Burton was eyed to direct at one point with Arnold Schwarzenegger considered for the Creature.

TEXAS CHAINSAW MASSACRE: THE NEXT GENERATION

Release Date	January 1, 1994 – August 29, 1997 (depending on location)
Budget	$600,000
Studio	Cinepix Film Properties, Colombia Pictures, Genre Pictures, Return Productions, Ultra Muchos Productions
Run Time	87 minutes (Theatrical cut), 94 minutes (Director's cut)
Sub-genre	Slasher
Source / Inspiration	Sequel
Writers	Kim Henkel, Tobe Hooper
Producers	Robert Kuhn, Kim Henkel, Genre Pictures, Return Productions, Ultra Muchos Productions
Directors	Kim Henkel
Box Office	$185, 898
Awards	---

Main Cast	
Actor / Actress	**Screen Names**

Renee Zellweger	Jenny
Matthew McConaughey	Vilmer
Robert Jacks	Leatherface Slaughter
Facts / More	
No one is massacred with a chainsaw in the film.	

1995

SPECIES	
Release Date	July 7, 1995
Budget	$35,000,000
Studio	MGM, Frank Mancuso Jr. Productions
Run Time	108 minutes
Sub-genre	Science Fiction
Source / Inspiration	---
Writers	Dennis Feldman
Producers	Frank Mancuso Jr., Dennis Feldman, Frank Mancuso Jr. Productions
Directors	Roger Donaldson
Box Office	$113,300,000
Awards	MTV Movie & TV Awards – MTV Movie Award
	Sci-Fi Universe Magazine, USA – Universal Reader's Choice Award
	Sitges – Catalonian International Film Festival – Best Special Effects

Main Cast	
Actor / Actress	**Screen Names**
Natasha Henstridge	Sil
Ben Kingsley	Xavier Fitch
Michael Madsen	Preston Lennox

Facts / More
SIL is actually S1L, the medical cell in the lab where the DNA is grown.

VILLAGE OF THE DAMNED	
Release Date	April 28, 1995
Budget	$22,000,000
Studio	Universal Pictures, Alphaville Films
Run Time	98 minutes
Sub-genre	---
Source / Inspiration	The Midwich Cuckoos (novel) by John Wyndham
Writers	David Himmelstein
Producers	Michael Preger, Sandy King, Alphaville Films
Directors	John Carpenter

Box Office	$9,400,000
Awards	---

Main Cast	
Actor / Actress	**Screen Names**
Christopher Reeve	Dr. Alan Chaffee
Kirstie Alley	Dr. Susan Verner
Mark Hamill	Reverend George
Meredith Salenger	Melanie Roberts

Facts / More

This was the final film of Christopher Reeves before a horse riding accident that left him paralyzed.

Two of the male children were played by female actresses.

TALES FROM THR CRYPT: DEMON KNIGHT

Release Date	January 13, 1995
Budget	$12,000,000
Studio	Universal Pictures, Crypt Keeper Productions
Run Time	92 minutes
Sub-genre	---
Source / Inspiration	Tales from the Crypt (Comic)
Writers	Ethan Reiff, Cyrus Voris, Mark Bishop
Producers	Gilbert Adler, Crypt Keeper Productions
Directors	Ernest Dickerson
Box Office	$21,100,000
Awards	Fangoria Chainsaw Awards – Chainsaw Award

Main Cast	
Actor / Actress	**Screen Names**
John Kassir	Crypt Keeper (voice)
Billy Zane	The Collector
Jada Pinkett Smith	Jeryline
William Sadler	Brayker

Facts / More

This is Billy Zane's favorite performance.

In the original draft of the movie Frank Brayker's character was named Silas. This is revealed in the novel adaptation which includes many scenes not in the movie as they would have inflated the budget. One potentially being where there were flying demons attacking the main cast during their time in the tunnels.

CANDYMAN: FAREWELL TO THE FLESH

Release Date	March 17, 1995
Budget	Unknown
Studio	Gramercy Pictures, Lava Productions
Run Time	95 minutes
Sub-genre	Supernatural, Slasher
Source / Inspiration	Sequel
Writers	Rand Ravich, Mark Kruger
Producers	Gregg Fienberg, Sigurjon Sighvatsson, Lava Productions
Directors	Bill Condon
Box Office	$13,900,000
Awards	---

Main Cast	
Actor / Actress	**Screen Names**
Tony Todd	Candyman / Daniel Robitaille
Kelly Rowan	Annie Tarrant
William O'Leary	Ethan Tarrant

Facts / More
The initial movie poster design showed a black man chasing a white woman. With the OJ Simpson case being public, this made the movie controversial and it was redesigned.

ICE CREAM MAN

Release Date	May 9, 1995
Budget	$2,000,000
Studio	A-Pix Entertainment Inc., Ardustry Home Entertainment LLC
Run Time	85 minutes
Sub-genre	---
Source / Inspiration	---
Writers	David Dobkin, Sven Davison
Producers	Paul Norman
Directors	Norman Apstein
Box Office	---
Awards	---

Main Cast	
Actor / Actress	**Screen Names**
Clint Howard	Gregory Tudor
Justin Isfeld	Johnny Spodak

| Anndi McAfee | Heather Langley |

Facts / More
The first draft of the script was written in 3 days.

HALLOWEEN: THE CURSE OF MICHAEL MYERS

Release Date	September 29, 1995
Budget	$5,000,000
Studio	Miramax Films, Dimension Films, Nightfall Productions, Trancas International
Run Time	88 minutes (Theatrical cut), 96 minutes (Producer's cut)
Sub-genre	Slasher
Source / Inspiration	Sequel
Writers	Daniel Farrands
Producers	Paul Freeman, Dimension Films, Nightfall Productions, Trancas International
Directors	Joe Chappelle
Box Office	$15,100,000
Awards	Academy of Science Fiction, Fantasy & Horror Films, USA – Saturn Award
	Fangoria Chainsaw Awards – Chainsaw Award
	The Stinkers Bad Movie Awards – Stinker Award

Main Cast	
Actor / Actress	**Screen Names**
Donald Pleasance	Dr. Sam Loomis
Marianne Hagan	Kara Strode
Paul Rudd	Tommy Doyle

Facts / More
Most of the cast and crew disowned this movie.
This was the only movie in the series to be shot in the fall. It was shot in Salt Lake City which got an early winter. This caused problems for the production team.

SCREAM	
Release Date	December 20, 1996
Budget	$15,000,000
Studio	Dimension Films, Woods Entertainment
Run Time	111 minutes
Sub-genre	Slasher / Mystery
Source / Inspiration	---
Writers	Kevin Williamson
Producers	Cathy Konrad, ary Woods, Woods Entertainment
Directors	Wes Craven
Box Office	$173,000,000
Awards	Academy of Science Fiction, Fantasy & Horror Films, USA – Saturn Awards
	ASCAP Film & Television Music Awards – ASCAP Award
	Fangoria Chainsaw Awards – Chainsaw Awards
	Gerardmer Film Festival – Grand Prize
	International Horror Guild – IHG Award
	MTV Movie & TV Awards – MTV Movie Award

Main Cast	
Actor / Actress	**Screen Names**
Drew Barrymore	Casey
Roger Jackson	Ghostface (phone voice)
Neve Campbell	Sidney
Courtney Cox	Gale Weathers
David Arquette	Deputy Dewey Riley
Skeet Ulrich	Billy Loomis
Matthew Lillard	Stuart
Rose McGowan	Tatum
Jamie Kennedy	Randy

Facts / More

The final house party sequence that's 42 minutes long was shot over 21 nights from sunset to sunrise. The crew had t-shirts made saying "I survived Scene 118" which they labeled the longest night in horror history.

When the principal opens his door after the mysterious knock, he walks into the hallway and sees a janitor. That is actually Wes Craven in a red and green striped sweater and a brown had to give a nod to A Nightmare on Elm Street.

FROM DUSK TILL DAWN

Release Date	January 17, 1996
Budget	$19,000,000
Studio	Miramax Films, Dimension Films, A Band Apart, Los Hooligans Productions
Run Time	108 minutes
Sub-genre	Supernatural
Source / Inspiration	---
Writers	Quentin Tarantino
Producers	Gianni Nunnari, Meir Teper, Dimension Films, A Band Apart, Los Hooligans Productions
Directors	Robert Rodriguez
Box Office	$59,300,000
Awards	Academy of Science Fiction, Fantasy & Horror Films, USA – Saturn Awards
	Amsterdam Fantastic Film Festival – Silver Scream Award
	Fangoria Chainsaw Awards – Chainsaw Awards
	MTV Movie & TV Awards – MTV Movie Award

Main Cast	
Actor / Actress	**Screen Names**
George Clooney	Seth Gecko
Quentin Tarantino	Richard Gecko
Harvey Keitel	Jacob Fuller
Juliette Lewis	Kate Fuller
Danny Trejo	Razor Charlie
Salma Hayek	Santanico Pandemonium
Fred Williamson	Frost

Facts / More
Salma Hayek spent two months with a therapist to get over her fear of snakes for her dance scene. She didn't have a choreographer as Robert Rodriguez told her to just dance to the music, a technique he used with Jessica Alba in Sin City (2005).
The Titty Twister was build in the desert in California.

HELLRAISER: BLOODLINE

Release Date	March 8, 1996
Budget	$4,000,000
Studio	Miramax Films, Dimension Films, Trans Atlantic Entertainment
Run Time	85 minutes

Sub-genre	---
Source / Inspiration	Sequel
Writers	Peter Atkins
Producers	Nancy Rae Stone, Dimension Films, Trans Atlantic Entertainment
Directors	Kevin Yagher
Box Office	$9,300,000
Awards	---

Main Cast	
Actor / Actress	**Screen Names**
Doug Bradley	Pinhead
Bruce Ramsey	Phillip / John / Paul
Valentina Vargas	Angelique

Facts / More
Guillermo Del Toro declined the chance of directing this film.

WISHMASTER	
Release Date	September 19,1997
Budget	$5,000,000
Studio	Live Entertainment, Pierre David
Run Time	90 minutes
Sub-genre	---
Source / Inspiration	---
Writers	Peter Atkins
Producers	Wes Craven
Directors	Robert Kurtzman
Box Office	$15,700,000
Awards	---

Main Cast	
Actor / Actress	**Screen Names**
Angus Scrimm	Narrator (voice)
Jake McKinnon	Skeleton Man
Greg Funk	Snake Man

Facts / More
One of the statues is the same statue used in Exoricst (1973).

I KNOW WHAT YOU DID LAST SUMMER	
Release Date	October 17, 1997
Budget	$17,000,000
Studio	Colombia Pictures, Mandalay Entertainment
Run Time	101 minutes
Sub-genre	Slasher
Source / Inspiration	I Know What You Did Last Summer (novel) by Lois Duncan
Writers	Kevin Williamson
Producers	Neal H. Moritz, Erik Feig, Stokely Chaffin, Mandalay Entertainment
Directors	Jim Gillespie
Box Office	$125,300,000
Awards	ASCAP Film & Television Music Awards – ASCAP Award

Blockbuster Entertainment Awards – Blockbuster Entertainment Award

Main Cast	
Actor / Actress	**Screen Names**
Jennifer Love Hewitt	Julie James
Freddie Prinze Jr.	Ray Bronson
Sarah Michelle Gellar	Helen Shivers
Ryan Phillippe	Barry Cox
Muse Watson	Ben Willis

Facts / More

Kevin Williamson wrote the screenplay before 1996, but was unable to sell it until his hug success with Scream (1996). Shortly after Scream's success, Colombia Picture snapped up the screen play for I Know What You Did last Summer.

Jennifer Love Hewitt isn't a fan of horror films. This and the sequel are the only horror films she's starred in.

Freddie Prinze Jr. and Sarah Michelle Gellar first met on the set of this film and later got married.

SCREAM II

Release Date	December 12, 1997
Budget	$24,000,000
Studio	Dimension Films, Konrad Pictures, Craven-Maddalena Films
Run Time	120 minutes
Sub-genre	Mystery
Source / Inspiration	Sequel
Writers	Kevin Williamson
Producers	Wes Craven, Kathy Konrad, Marianne Maddalena, Konrad Pictures, Craven-Maddalena Films
Directors	Wes Craven
Box Office	$172,400,000
Awards	ASCAP Film & Television Music Awards – ASCAP Award
	Blockbuster Entertainment Awards – Blockbuster Entertainment Award
	Fangoria Chainsaw Awards – Chainsaw Award
	MTV Movie & TV Awards – MTV Movie Award

Main Cast	
Actor / Actress	**Screen Names**
Neve Campbell	Sidney Prescott
Courtney Cox	Gale Weathers
Elise Neal	Hallie
David Arquette	Dewey Riley

Timothy Olyphant	Micky
Jerry O'Connell	Derek
Laurie Metcalf	Debbi Salt (Mrs Loomis)
Liev Schreiber	Cotton Weary
Facts / More	
The movie earned over $100,000,000 in its opening weekend.	
Denise Richards was offered a role, but was working on Starship Troopers.	
Toby Maguire was offered the role of Mickey.	

AN AMERICAN WEREWOLF IN PARIS

Release Date	August 31, 1997 (UK), December 25, 1997 (USA)
Budget	$25,000,000
Studio	Buena Vista Pictures, Hollywood Pictures, Stonewood Productions
Run Time	102 minutes
Sub-genre	Supernatural
Source / Inspiration	John Landis
Writers	Tim Berns, Tom Stern, Anthony Waller
Producers	Richard Claus
Directors	Anthony Waller
Box Office	$26,600,000
Awards	Gerardmer Film Festival – Audience Award, Fun Trophy, Grand Prize

Main Cast	
Actor / Actress	**Screen Names**
Tom Everett Scott	Andy McDermott
Julie Delpy	Serafine Pigot
Phil Buckman	Chris
Facts / More	
This film was in development for six years.	

THE DEVIL'S ADVOCATE

Release Date	October 17, 1997
Budget	$57,000,000
Studio	Warner Bros. Pictures, Regency Enterprises
Run Time	144 minutes
Sub-genre	Supernatural

Source / Inspiration	The Devil's Advocate (novel) by Andrew Neiderman
Writers	Jonathan Lemkin, Tony Gilroy
Producers	Arnon Milchan, Arnold Kopelson, Anne Kopelson, Regency Enterprise
Directors	Taylor Hackford
Box Office	$153,000,000
Awards	Academy of Science Fiction, Fantasy & Horror Films, USA – Saturn Award Fangoria Chainsaw Awards – Chainsaw Award

Main Cast	
Actor / Actress	**Screen Names**
Keanu Reeves	Levin Lomax
Al Pacino	John Milton
Charlize Theron	Mary Ann Lomax

Facts / More
Al Pacino declind the role thre times before finally taking the part.

ANACONDA

Release Date	April 11, 1997
Budget	$45,000,000
Studio	Sony Pictures Releasing, Columbia Pictures, Cinema Line Film Corporation
Run Time	89 minutes
Sub-genre	---
Source / Inspiration	---
Writers	Hans Bauer, Jim Cash, Jack Epps Jr.
Producers	Verna Harrah, Carol Little, Leonard Rabinowitz, Columbia Pictures, Cinema Line Film Corporation
Directors	Luis Llosa
Box Office	$136,800,000
Awards	ALMA Awards – ALMA Award BMI Film & TV Awards – BMI Award The Stinkers Bad Movie Awards – Stinker Award World Animation Celebration – WAC Winner

Main Cast	
Actor / Actress	**Screen Names**
Jennifer Lopez	Terri Flores
Ice Cube	Danny Rich
Jon Voight	Paul Serone
Owen Wilson	Gary Dixon

| Danny Trejo | Poacher |
| Frank Welker | Anaconda (voice) |

Facts / More
The CGI for the anacondas cost $100,000 per second.
The anacondas attack humans, but not each other. In real life, anacondas are cannibalistic.

1998

HALLOWEEN H20: 20 YEARS LATER

Release Date	August 5, 1998
Budget	$17,000,000
Studio	Miramax Films, Dimension Films, Nightfall Productions, Trancas International
Run Time	86 minutes
Sub-genre	Slasher
Source / Inspiration	Sequel
Writers	Robert Zappia, Matt Greenberg
Producers	Paul Freeman, Dimension Films, Nightfall Productions, Trancas International
Directors	Steve Miner
Box Office	$75,000,000
Awards	Academy of Science Fiction, Fantasy & Horror Films, USA – Saturn Award
	Fangoria Chainsaw Awards – Chainsaw Award

Main Cast	
Actor / Actress	**Screen Names**
Jamie Lee Curtis	Laurie Straud / Keri Tate
Chris Durand	Michael Myers
Josh Hartnett	John
Jodi Lyn O'Keefe	Sarah
Adam Hann-Byrd	Charlie
Michelle Williams	Molly
LL Cool J	Ronny
Janet Leigh	Norma

Facts / More
The first Halloween film with Jamie Lee Curtis, but not Donald Pleasance.

I STILL KNOW WHAT YOU DID LAST SUMMER

Release Date	November 13, 1998
Budget	$24,000,000
Studio	Sony Pictures Releasing, Colombia Pictures, Mandalay Entertainment, Estudios Churubuso
Run Time	101 minutes
Sub-genre	Slasher

Source / Inspiration	Sequel
Writers	Trey Callaway
Producers	Neal H. Moritz, Erik Feig, Stokely Chaffin, William S. Beasley, Colombia Pictures, Mandalay Entertainment, Estudios Churubuso
Directors	Danny Cannon
Box Office	$84,000,000
Awards	Blockbuster Entertainment Awards – Blockbuster Entertainment Award
	Fangoria Chainsaw Awards – Chainsaw Award
	Teen Choice Awards – Teen Choice Award
	The Stinkers Bad Movie Awards – Stinker Award

Main Cast	
Actor / Actress	**Screen Names**
Jennifer Love Hewitt	Julie James
Freddie Prinze Jr.	Ray Bronson
Brandy Norwood	Karla Wilson
Mekhi Phifer	Tyrell
Muse Watson	Ben Willis
Matthew Settle	Will Benson

Facts / More
Due to the negative reaction from critics upon its release, Freddie Prinze Jr. claims he has never seen the film.
If you break up the surnames "Willis" and "Benson", it means Will is Ben's son.

BLADE

Release Date	August 21, 1998
Budget	$45,000,000
Studio	New Line Cinema, Marvel Enterprises, Amen Ra Films, Imaginary Forces
Run Time	120 minutes
Sub-genre	Supernatural
Source / Inspiration	Blade (comic)
Writers	David S. Goyer
Producers	Peter Frankfurt, Wesley Snipes, Robert Engelman, Marvel Enterprises, Amen Ra Films, Imaginary Forces
Directors	Stephen Norrington
Box Office	$131,200,000
Awards	ASCAP Film & Television Music Awards – ASCAP Award
	Blockbuster Entertainment Awards – Blockbuster Award
	Fangoria Chainsaw Awards – Chainsaw Award

	MTV Movie & TV Awards – MTV Movie Award

Main Cast	
Actor / Actress	**Screen Names**
Wesley Snipes	Blade
Stephen Dorff	Deacon Frost
Kris Kristofferson	Whistler
N'Bushe Wright	Karen

Facts / More
Jet Li was offered the part of Deacon Frost, but opted to do Lethal Weapon 4.

DEEP RISING

Release Date	January 30, 1998
Budget	$45,000,000
Studio	Buena Vista Pictures, Cinergi Productions, Hollywood Pictures, Cinergi Pictures
Run Time	106 minutes
Sub-genre	---
Source / Inspiration	---
Writers	Stephen Sommers
Producers	John Baldecchi, Mario Iscovich, Laurence Mark, Hollywood Pictures, Cinergi Pictures
Directors	Stephen Sommers
Box Office	$11,200,000
Awards	---

Main Cast	
Actor / Actress	**Screen Names**
Treat Williams	John Finnegan
Famke Janssen	Trillian St. James
Anthony Heald	Simon Canton

Facts / More
Deep Rising was released one month after Titanic.
Anthony Heald shot his death scene first.

VAMPIRES

Release Date	October 30, 1998
Budget	$20,000,000
Studio	Sony Pictures Releasing, Colombia Pictures, Film Office, JVC Entertainment Networks,

	Largo Entertainment, Spooky Tooth Productions, Storm King Productions
Run Time	108 minutes
Sub-genre	Supernatural
Source / Inspiration	Vampires (novel) by John Steakley
Writers	Don Jakoby
Producers	Sandy King, Colombia Pictures, Film Office, JVC Entertainment Networks, Largo Entertainment, Spooky Tooth Productions, Storm King Productions
Directors	John Carpenter
Box Office	$20,300,000
Awards	Academy of Science Fiction, Fantasy & Horror Films, USA – Saturn Award Fangoria Chainsaw Awards – Chainsaw Award The Stinkers Bad Movie Awards – Stinker Award

Main Cast	
Actor / Actress	**Screen Names**
James Woods	Jack Crow
Daniel Baldwin	Anthony Montoya

Facts / More
The only film in the 90s that was a financial success for John Carpenter.

BRIDE OF CHUCKY

Release Date	October 16, 1998
Budget	$25,000,000
Studio	Universal Pictures, David Kirschner Productions
Run Time	89 minutes
Sub-genre	Slasher
Source / Inspiration	Sequel
Writers	Don Mancini
Producers	David Kirschner, Grace Gilroy, David Kirschner Productions
Directors	Ronny Yu
Box Office	$50,700,000
Awards	Academy of Science Fiction, Fantasy & Horror Films, USA – Saturn Award Fangoria Chainsaw Awards – Chainsaw Award Fantafestival – Best Actress, Best Special Effects Gerardmer Film Festival – Special Jury Prize

Main Cast	
Actor / Actress	**Screen Names**
Jennifer Tilly	Tiffany

Brad Dourif	Chucky (voice)
Katherine Heigl	Jade
Nick Stabile	Jesse
Facts / More	

This is Brad Dourif's favorite Chucky movie.

According to Jennifer Tilly, the se doll scene was all improvised.

Chucky kills Tiffany twice in this movie. Once when she's human and again towards the end when she's a doll.

BLAIR WITCH PROJECT	
Release Date	July 14, 1999
Budget	$500,000
Studio	Artisan Entertainment, Haxan Films
Run Time	81 minutes
Sub-genre	Supernatural
Source / Inspiration	---
Writers	Daniel Myrick, Eduardo Sanchez
Producers	Gregg Hale, Robin Cowie
Directors	Daniel Myrick, Eduardo Sanchez
Box Office	$248,600,000
Awards	Cannes Film Festival – Award of the Youth
	Csapnivalo Awards – Golden Slate
	Fangoria Chainsaw Awards – Chainsaw Award
	Film Independent Spirit Awards – Independent Spirit Award
	Florida Film Critics Circle Awards – Golden Orange Award
	Golden Trailer Awards – Golden Trailer
	Online Film & Television Association – OFTA Film Award
	Online Film Critics Society Awards – OFCS Award
	PGA Awards – Nova Award
	Puchon International Fantastic Film Festival – Netizen's Choice Award
	Razzie Awards – Razzie Award
	Sitges – Catalonian International Film Festival – Special Mention
	The Stinkers Bad Movie Awards – Stinker Award
	Yoga Awards – Yoga Award

Main Cast	
Actor / Actress	**Screen Names**
---	---

Facts / More
Shooting The Blair Witch Project was completed in a total of 8 days.

HOUSE ON HAUNTED HILL

Release Date	October 29, 1999
Budget	$19,000,000
Studio	Warner Bros., Dark Castle Entertainment
Run Time	93 minutes
Sub-genre	Supernatural
Source / Inspiration	Remake of House on Haunted Hill (1959)
Writers	Dick Beebe
Producers	Robert Zemeckis, Joel Silver, Gilbert Adler, Terry A. Castle, Dark Castle Entertainment
Directors	William Malone
Box Office	$40,800,000
Awards	Blockbuster Entertainment Awards – Blockbuster Award

Main Cast	
Actor / Actress	**Screen Names**
Geoffrey Rush	Stephen Price
Famke Janssen	Evelyn
Taye Diggs	Eddie
Ali Larter	Sara
Jeffrey Combs	Dr. Vannacutt

Facts / More
Th director of the original and the remake are both named William.
Marilyn Manson was considered for the role of Dr. Vannacutt.

THE SIXTH SENSE

Release Date	August 6, 1999
Budget	$40,000,000
Studio	Buena Vista Pictures Distribution, Hollywood Pictures, Spyglass Entertainment, The Kennedy/Marshall Company, Barry Mendel Productions
Run Time	107 minutes
Sub-genre	Supernatural
Source / Inspiration	---
Writers	M. Night Shyamalan
Producers	Frank Marshall, Kathleen Kennedy, Barry Mendel, Hollywood Pictures, Spyglass Entertainment, The Kennedy/Marshall Company, Barry Mendel Productions
Directors	M. Night Shyamalan

Box Office	$672,800,000
Awards	Academy of Science Fiction, Fantasy & Horror Films, USA – Saturn Award
	ASCAP Film & Television Music Awards – ASCAP Award
	Awards of the Japanese Academy – Award of the Japanese Academy
	Blockbuster Entertainment Awards – Blockbuster Entertainment Award
	Bogey Awards, Germany – Bogey Award in Gold
	Bram Stoker Awards – Bram Stoker Award
	Broadcast Film Critics Association Awards – Critics Choice Award
	Cannes Film Festival – DVD Design Award
	Dallas-Fort Worth Film Critics Association Awards – DFWFCA Award
	Empire Awards UK – Empire Award
	Fangoria Chainsaw Awards – Chainsaw Award
	Florida Film Critics Circle Awards – FFCC Award
	Golden Screen, Germany – Golden Screen Award
	Kansas City Film Critics Circle Awards – KCFCC Award
	Las Vegas Film Critics Society Awards – Sierra Award
	MTV Movie & TV Awards – MTV Movie Award
	Online Film & Television Association – OFTA Film Award
	Online Film Critics Society Awards – OFCS Award
	People's Choice Awards, USA – People's Choice Award
	Satellite Awards – Golden Satellite Award
	Science Fiction & Fantasy Writers of America – Nebula Award
	Southeastern Film Critics Association Awards – SEFCA Award
	Teen Choice Awards – Teen Choice Award
	Young Artist Awards – Young Artist Award
	YoungStar Awards – YoungStar Award

Main Cast

Actor / Actress	Screen Names
Bruce Willis	Malcolm Crow
Haley Joe Osment	Cole Sear
Toni Collette	Lyn Sear

Facts / More

The Sixth Sense is references in future movies including 50 First Dates (2004) where forgetful Lucy gave the VHS to her father as a birthday gift and the family have to rewatch it every night as Lucy's memory resets.

The Sixth Sense was the second highest grossing film of 1999 behind Star Wars – Episode I: The Phantom Menace.

STIGMATA

Release Date	September 10, 1999
Budget	$29,000,000
Studio	MGM, FGM Entertainment
Run Time	103 minutes
Sub-genre	Supernatural
Source / Inspiration	---
Writers	Tom Lazarus, Rick Ramage
Producers	Frank Mancuso, Jr., FGM Entertainment
Directors	Rupert Wainwright
Box Office	$89,400,000
Awards	---

Main Cast	
Actor / Actress	**Screen Names**
Patricia Arquette	Frankie Paige
Gabriel Byrne	Father Andrew Kiernan
Nia Long	Donna Chadway
Jonathan Pryce	Cardinal Daniel Houseman
Thomas Kopache	Father Durning

Facts / More
During the subway scene there's actually footage from Money Train (1995).
The Aramaic that Frankie writes on the wall is actually Ancient Hebrew because the director thought it looked more "intriguing".
Aramaic originated in ancient Syria and is referred to as the ancient language of the dead in many books and TV shows including *The New England Vampire* and *The Vampire Diaries*.

2000

FINAL DESTINATION	
Release Date	March 17, 2000
Budget	$23,000,000
Studio	New Line Cinema, Zide/Perry Productions, Hard Eight Pictures
Run Time	98 minutes
Sub-genre	Supernatural
Source / Inspiration	Jeffrey Reddick (story)
Writers	Glen Morgan, James Wong, Jeffrey Reddick
Producers	Warren Zide, Craig Perry, Glen Morgan, Zide/Perry Productions, Hard Eight Pictures
Directors	James Wong
Box Office	$112,900,000
Awards	Academy of Science Fiction, Fantasy & Horror Films, USA – Saturn Award
	Young Hollywood Awards – Young Hollywood Award

Main Cast	
Actor / Actress	**Screen Names**
Devon Sawa	Alex Browning
Ali Larter	Clear Rivers
Kerr Smith	Carter Horton
Kristen Cloke	Valerie Lewton
Tony Todd	Bludworth

Facts / More
The Chinese title translates to "The Death God Comes".
The story was originally an abandoned X-Files script.
While Alex is reading a magazine in his room an owl lands on the tree outside. In many cultures an owl is considered an Omen of death. Alex then throws the magazine to get the "Tod" message land on his knee.

AMERICAN PSYCHO	
Release Date	April 14, 2000
Budget	$7,000,000
Studio	Lions Gate Films, Colombia Pictures, Edward R. Pressman Productions, Muse Productions
Run Time	101 minutes
Sub-genre	Slasher

Source / Inspiration	American Psycho (novel) by Bret Easton Ellis
Writers	Mary Harron, Guinevere Turner
Producers	Edwaard R. Pressman, Chris Hanley, Christian Halsey Solomon, Edward R. Pressman Productions, Muse Productions
Directors	Mary Harron
Box Office	$34,300,000
Awards	Awards Circuit Community Awards – ACCA
	Chlotrudis Awards – Chlotrudis Award
	Fangoria Chainsaw Awards – Chainsaw Award
	Faro Island Film Festival – Golden Train Award
	International Horror Guild – IHG Award
	National Board of Review, USA – Special Recognition

Main Cast	
Actor / Actress	**Screen Names**
Christian Bale	Patrick Bateman
Jared Leto	Paul Allen
Reese Witherspoon	Evelyn Williams
Willem Dafoe	Donald Kimball
Justin Theroux	Timothy Bryce

Facts / More
When Christian Bale spoke in his native British accent after the wrap party, the crew didn't know he was speaking with an American accent the whole time as he would even speak in an American accent off screen.
Ewan McGregor was offered the role of Patrick Bateman, but declined after Christian Bale urged him to do so. Tom Hardy also mentioned in a Dark Knight Rises interview that Christian Bale was someone you probably wouldn't want to mess with in real life and this could have been more persuasive for McGregor.

WHAT LIES BENEATH

Release Date	July 21, 2000
Budget	$100,000,000
Studio	DreamWorks Pictures, 20th Century Fox, ImageMovers
Run Time	130 minutes
Sub-genre	---
Source / Inspiration	Sarah Kernochan (story)
Writers	Clark Gregg
Producers	Jack Rapke, Robert Zemeckis, Steve Starkey, ImageMovers
Directors	Robert Zemeckis
Box Office	$291,400,000
Awards	ASCAP Film & Television Music Awards – ASCAP Award

	Blockbuster Entertainment Awards – Blockbuster Entertainment Award
	Il Film Festival Nazionale del Doppiaggio Voci nell'Ombra – Audience Awards, Film Award
	Italian National Syndicate of Film Journalists – Silver Ribbon
	Yoga Awards – Yoga Award

Main Cast	
Actor / Actress	**Screen Names**
Michelle Pfeiffer	Claire Spencer
Harrison Ford	Norman Spencer
Katharine Towne	Caitlin Spencer

Facts / More
Robert Zemeckis film this while production on Cast Away was paused (so Tom Hanks could lose weight for the future island sequence).

SCREAM 3

Release Date	February 4, 2000
Budget	$40,000,000
Studio	Dimension Films, Konrad Pictures, Craven/Maddalena Films
Run Time	117 minutes
Sub-genre	Slasher / Mystery
Source / Inspiration	Sequel
Writers	Ehren Kruger
Producers	Cathy Konrad, Kevin Williamson, Marianne Maddalena, Konrad Pictures, Craven/Maddalena Films
Directors	Wes Craven
Box Office	$161,800,000
Awards	Blockbuster Entertainment Awards – Blockbuster Entertainment Award
	Bogey Awards, Germany – Bogey Award
	Fangoria Chainsaw Awards – Chainsaw Award
	International Monitor Awards – Monitor Award
	Teen Choice Awards – Teen Choice Award

Main Cast	
Actor / Actress	**Screen Names**
Liev Schreiber	Cotton Weary
Neve Campbell	Sidney Prescott
Courtney Cox Arquette	Gale Weathers
Scott Foley	Roman Bridger

David Arquette	Dewey Riley
Kelly Rutherford	Christine
Rogr Jackson	Ghostface (voice)
Facts / More	
Wes Craven filmed three different endings and didn't tell the cast which one he was going to use. Journalists weren't allowed to know anything until two days before the film's release. This was to keep the plot twists a secret.	

GINGERSNAPS

Release Date	August 1, 2000 (Munich), May 11, 2001
Budget	$4,500,000
Studio	Motion International
Run Time	108 minutes
Sub-genre	---
Source / Inspiration	---
Writers	Karen Walton, John Fawcett
Producers	Karen Lee Hall, Steve Hoban
Directors	John Fawcett
Box Office	$572,781
Awards	Academy of Science Fiction, Fantasy & Horror Films, USA – Saturn Award Canadian Comedy Awards – Canadian Comedy Awards Fangoria Chainsaw Awards – Chainsaw Award International Horror Guild – IHG Award Malaga International Week of Fantastic Cinema – Best Actress, Best Film, Best Special Effects Toronto International Film Festival – Best Canadian Feature Film

Main Cast	
Actor / Actress	**Screen Names**
Emily Perkins	Brigitte
Katharine Isabelle	Ginger
Mimi Rogers	Pamela
Kris Lemche	Sam
Facts / More	
Initially banned from certain cinemas in the UK, labelled as promoting teen violence, but its VHS release a few month later became one of the fastest selling horror films.	

JEEPERS CREEPERS

Release Date	August 31, 2001
Budget	$10,000,000
Studio	United Artists, MGM, American Zoetrope, Cinerenta-Cinerbeta, Cinerenta Medienbeteiligungs KG
Run Time	91 minutes
Sub-genre	---
Source / Inspiration	---
Writers	Victor Salva
Producers	J. Todd Harris, Barry Opper, Tom Luse, American Zoetrope, Cinerenta-Cinerbeta, Cinerenta Medienbeteiligungs KG
Directors	Victor Salva
Box Office	$59,000,000
Awards	Crystal Reel Awards – Crystal Reel Award
	Fangoria Chainsaw Awards – Chainsaw Award
	Fright Meter Awards – Fright Meter Award

Main Cast

Actor / Actress	Screen Names
Justin Long	Darry
Gina Philips	Trish
Jonathan Breck	The Creeper

Facts / More

This film was inspired by the real life crimes of Dennis Depue and the area he disposed of his wife's body was strikingly similar to the locations in the movie.

HANNIBAL

Release Date	February 9, 2001
Budget	$87,000,000
Studio	MGM, Universal Pictures, Dino De Laurentiis, Scott Free Productions
Run Time	132 minutes
Sub-genre	---
Source / Inspiration	Sequel
Writers	David Mamet, Steven Zaillian
Producers	Dino De Laurentiis, Martha De Laurentiis, Ridley Scott, MGM, Universal Pictures, Dino

	De Laurentiis, Scott Free Productions
Directors	Ridley Scott
Box Office	$351,600,000
Awards	Academy of Science Fiction, Fantasy & Horror Films, USA – Saturn Award
	ASCAP Film & Television Music Awards – ASCAP Award
	Bogey Awards, Germany – Bogey Award
	Fangoria Chainsaw Awards – Chainsaw Award
	Golden Screen, Germany – Golden Screen
	GoldSpirit Awards – GoldSpirit Award
	Italian National Syndicate of Film Journalists – Silver Ribbon
	Jupiter Awards – Jupiter Award

Main Cast	
Actor / Actress	**Screen Names**
Anthony Hopkins	Hannibal Lecter
Julianne Moore	Clarice Starling
Gary Oldman	Mason Verger

Facts / More
Gary Oldman spent 5 hours a day in the make-up chair.
Jodie Foster declined the chance to return as Clarice Starling due to the violence in the novel.

THIR13EN GHOSTS [THIRTEEN GHOSTS]

Release Date	October 26, 2001
Budget	$42,000,0000
Studio	Warner Bros., Colombia TriStar, Dark Castle Entertainment
Run Time	91 minutes
Sub-genre	---
Source / Inspiration	13 Ghosts (1960 movie)
Writers	Neal Marshall Stevens, Richard D'Ovidio
Producers	Robert Zemeckis, Joel Silver, Gilbert Adler, Warner Bros., Colombia TriStar, Dark Castle Entertainment
Directors	Steve Beck
Box Office	$68,500,000
Awards	Fangoria Chainsaw Awards – Chainsaw Award

Main Cast	
Actor / Actress	**Screen Names**
Tony Shalhoub	Arthur Kriticos

Embeth Davidtz	Kalina Oretzia
Matthew Lillard	Dennis Rafkin
Facts / More	
Excluding the opening scene, the entire movie takes place over the course of a day.	

JASON X

Release Date	November 2001 (Spain), April 26, 2002
Budget	$14,000,000
Studio	New Line Cinema, Crystal Lake Entertainment, Friday X Productions
Run Time	92 minutes
Sub-genre	---
Source / Inspiration	Sequel
Writers	Todd Farmer
Producers	Noel Cunningham, Crystal Lake Entertainment, Friday X Productions
Directors	Jim Isaac
Box Office	$17,100,000
Awards	---
Main Cast	
Actor / Actress	**Screen Names**
Kane Hodder	Jason Vorhees
Facts / More	
This was the first film in the series to rely on digital effects for gore shots.	

DOG SOLDIERS

Release Date	May 10, 2002
Budget	£2,300,000
Studio	Pathe, Kismet Entertainment Group, The Noel Gay Motion Picture Company, Victor Film Company, Carousel Picture Company
Run Time	105 minutes
Sub-genre	Supernatural
Source / Inspiration	---
Writers	Neil Marshall
Producers	Christopher Figg, Tom Reeve, David E. Allen, Kismet Entertainment Group, The Noel Gay Motion Picture Company, Victor Film Company, Carousel Picture Company
Directors	Neil Marshall
Box Office	£5,000,000
Awards	Academy of Science Fiction, Fantasy & Horror Films, USA – Saturn Award
	BIFFF – Golden Raven, Pegsus Audience Award
	Cinenygma – Luxembourg International Film Festival
	Fangoria Chainsaw Awards – Chainsaw Award

Main Cast

Actor / Actress	Screen Names
Sean Pertwee	Sergeant Wells
Kevin McKidd	Cooper
Emma Cleasby	Megan
Liam Cunningham	Ryan
Darren Mirfitt	Spoon

Facts / More

The line "there is no Spoon" is a nod to The Matrix.

All the visual are actually practical, not CGI. The werewolf actors would stand on angled stilts which they claimed was very uncomfortable.

This was Neil Marshall's first feature film. He admitted that a sequel was unlikely. He doesn't own the rights anymore.

GHOST SHIP

Release Date	October 25, 2002
Budget	$20,000,000

Studio	Warner Bros. Pictures, Dark Castle Entertainment, Village Roadshow Pictures, NPV Entertainment
Run Time	90 minutes
Sub-genre	Supernatural
Source / Inspiration	Mary Celeste Ghost Ship
Writers	Mark Hanlon, John Pogue
Producers	Joel Silver, Robert Zemeckis, Gilbert Adler
Directors	Steve Beck
Box Office	$68,300,000
Awards	---

Main Cast	
Actor / Actress	**Screen Names**
Gabriel Byrne	Murphy
Julianna Marguiles	Epps
Ron Eldard	Dodge
Karl Urban	Munder
Francesca Rettondini	Francesca

Facts / More
In 2016, the opening scene was named one of the greatest in horror history by ComingSoon.
The opening scene was initially meant to be all the characters being beheaded, but the studio deemed it too graphic and decided to severe the torso.

HALLOWEEN: RESURRECTION

Release Date	July 12, 2002
Budget	$15,000,000
Studio	Dimension Films, Miramax Films, Nightfall Productions, Trancas Interactions Films
Run Time	90 minutes
Sub-genre	Slasher
Source / Inspiration	Sequel
Writers	Larry Brand, Sean Hood
Producers	Paul Freeman
Directors	Rick Rosenthal
Box Office	$37,600,000
Awards	Academy of Science Fiction, Fantasy & Horror Films, USA – Saturn Award

Main Cast	
Actor / Actress	**Screen Names**
Jamie Lee Curtis	Laurie Strode

Brad Loree	Michael Myers
Busta Rhymes	Freddie Harris
Facts / More	
John Carpenter has stated that this movie makes him cringe.	
Jamie Lee Curtis allegedly called this film "a joke".	

CABIN FEVER

Release Date	September 14, 2002 (TIFF), September 12, 2003
Budget	$1,500,000
Studio	Lions Gate Films, Black Sky Entertainment, Deer Path Films, Down Home Entertainment, Tonic Films
Run Time	94 minutes
Sub-genre	---
Source / Inspiration	---
Writers	Eli Roth, Randy Pearlstein
Producers	Lauren Moews, Sam Froelich, Evan Astrowsky, Eli Roth, Deer Path Films, Down Home Entertainment, Tonic Films
Directors	Eli Roth
Box Office	$30,600,000
Awards	Fangoria Chainsaw Awards – Chainsaw Award
	Shockfest Film Festival, USA – Shocker Award of the Year
	Sitges – Catalonian International Film Festival – Best Make-Up

Main Cast	
Actor / Actress	**Screen Names**
Rider Strong	Paul
Jordan Ladd	Karen
Cerina Vincent	Marcy
Facts / More	
As the film progresses, the light levels become increasingly darker.	

28 DAYS LATER

Release Date	November 1, 2002
Budget	$8,000,000
Studio	Fox Searchlight Pictures, DNA Films, UK Film Council
Run Time	113 minutes
Sub-genre	---

Source / Inspiration	---
Writers	Alex Garland
Producers	Andrew MacDonald, DNA Films, UK Film Council
Directors	Danny Boyle
Box Office	$85,700,000
Awards	Academy of Science Fiction, Fantasy & Horror Films, USA – Saturn Award
	Black Reels Awards – Black Reel
	Empire Awards, UK – Empire Award
	European Film Awards – European Film Awards
	Fangoria Chainsaw Awards – Chainsaw Award
	Fantasport – Grand Prize of European Fantasy Film in Silver, International Fantasy Film Award
	Golden Schmoes Awards – Golden Schmoes
	Neuchatel International Fantastic Film Festival – Narcisse Award

Main Cast	
Actor / Actress	**Screen Names**
Alex Palmer	Activist
Bindu De Stoppani	Activist
David Schneider	Scientist

Facts / More
Stephen King bought out an entire showing of the film in New York City.
One of the first mainstream films to be shot digitally instead of with film.

THE RING

Release Date	October 18, 2002
Budget	$48,000,000
Studio	DreamWorks Pictures, MacDonald/Parkes Productions, BenderSpink, Inc.
Run Time	115 minutes
Sub-genre	Supernatural
Source / Inspiration	Ring (1998 horror film, Japan)
Writers	Ehren Kruger
Producers	Walter F. Parkes, Laurie MacDonald, MacDonald/Parkes Productions, BenderSpink, Inc.
Directors	Gore Verbinski
Box Office	$249,400,000
Awards	Science Fiction, Fantasy & Horror Films, USA – Saturn Award
	ASCAP Film & Television Music Awards – ASCAP Award

	Fangoria Chainsaw Awards – Chainsaw Award
	Golden Schmoes Awards – Golden Schmoes
	Golden Trailer Awards – Golden Trailer
	Hollywood Film Awards – Hollywood Breakthrough Award
	MTV Movie & TV Awards – MTV Movie Award
	Teen Choice Awards – Teen Choice Award

Main Cast	
Actor / Actress	**Screen Names**
Naomi Watts	Rachel
Martin Henderson	Noah
David Dorfman	Aidan
Brian Cox	Richard Morgan

Facts / More
The killer video was used a commercial for a year before the film as mentioned.
This was the highest grossing horror remake in history until 2017 when Stephen King's It surpassed it.
The Ring sold more than 2 million copies in its first 24 hours of release on DVD.
Jennifer Love Hewitt was offered the part of Rachel, but declined as she didn't want to be a "scream queen".

QUEEN OF THE DAMNED

Release Date	February 22, 2002
Budget	$35,000,000
Studio	Warner Bros. Pictures, Village Roadshow Pictures, NPV Entertainment, Material Productions
Run Time	101 minutes
Sub-genre	Supernatural
Source / Inspiration	The Vampire Chronicles (novel) Anne Rice
Writers	Scott Abbott, Michael Petroni
Producers	Jorge Saralegui, Village Roadshow Pictures, NPV Entertainment, Material Productions
Directors	Michael Rymer
Box Office	$45,500,000
Awards	---

Main Cast	
Actor / Actress	**Screen Names**
Aaliyah	Queen Akasha
Stuart Townsend	Lestat
Vincent Perez	Marius

BLADE II

Release Date	March 22, 2002
Budget	$54,000,000
Studio	New Line Cinema, Marvel Enterprises, Amen Ra Films, Imaginary Forces
Run Time	117 minutes
Sub-genre	Supernatural
Source / Inspiration	Sequel
Writers	Marv Wolfman, Gene Colan, David S. Goyer
Producers	Peter Frankfurt, Wesley Snipes, Patrick Palmer, Marvel Enterprises, Amen Ra Films, Imaginary Forces
Directors	Guillermo Del Toro
Box Office	$155,000,000
Awards	ASCAP Film & Television Music Awards – ASCAP Awards Black Reel Awards – Black Reel Bogey Awards, Germany – Bogey Awards Fangoria Chainsaw Awards – Chainsaw Awards MTV Movie Awards, Latina America – MTV Movie Award World Stunt Awards – Taurus Award

Main Cast	
Actor / Actress	**Screen Names**
Wesley Snipes	Blade
Kris Kristofferson	Whistler
Ron Pearlman	Reinhardt

Facts / More
The body count is 110.
Over 30 of the crew were blinded by the misuse of UV lights during th autopsy scene.
This is the only movie in the Blade trilogy that used its original written ending. Blade and Blade: Trinity went through reshoots to improve the climax.

JU-ON: THE GRUDGE

Release Date	18 October, 2002
Budget	500,000,000 (JPY)
Studio	Lions Gate Films, Pioneer LDC, Nikkatsu, Oz Co., Xanaduex
Run Time	92 minutes
Sub-genre	Supernatural
Source / Inspiration	---
Writers	Takashi Shimizu
Producers	Taka Ichise
Directors	Takashi Shimizu
Box Office	$3,657,000
Awards	Screamfest – Festival Trophy

Main Cast	
Actor / Actress	**Screen Names**
Megumi Okina	Rika Nishina
Misaki Ito	Hitomi Tokunaga
Misa Uehara	Izumi Toyama

Facts / More
The is actually the third installment in the Ju-On series. Ju-On: The Curse (2000) and Ju-On: The Curse 2 (2000). Both were low budget and not as successful.

RED DRAGON

Release Date	October 4, 2002
Budget	$78,000,000
Studio	Universal Pictures, Imagine Corporation
Run Time	124 minutes
Sub-genre	---
Source / Inspiration	Red Dragon (novel) by Thomas Harris
Writers	Ted Tally
Producers	Dino De Laurentiis, Martha De Laurentiis, Universal Pictures, Imagine Corporation
Directors	Brett Ratner
Box Office	$209,200,000
Awards	Fangoria Chainsaw Awards – Chainsaw Award
	London Critics Circle Film Awards – ALFS Award
	World Stunt Awards – Taurus Award
	Young Artist Awards – Young Artist Award

Main Cast

Actor / Actress	Screen Names
Anthony Hopkins	Dr. Hannibal Lecter
Edward Norton	Will Graham
Ralph Fiennes	Francis Dolarhyde
Emily Watson	Reba McClane
Mary-Louise Parker	Molly Graham
Facts / More	
Many of Hannibal's lines are exactly the same as Dr. Bloom's in the book.	
Anthony Hopkins lost 20 pounds to play a younger Hannibal.	
Michael Bay was offered the chance to direct.	

WRONG TURN	
Release Date	May 30, 2003
Budget	$12,600,000
Studio	20th Century Fox, Constantin Film, Summit Entertainment, Regency Enterprises
Run Time	84 minutes
Sub-genre	---
Source / Inspiration	---
Writers	Alan McElroy
Producers	Stan Winston, Brian Gilbert, Erik Feig, Robert Kulzer, Constantin Film, Summit Entertainment, Regency Enterprises
Directors	Rob Schmidt
Box Office	$28,700,000
Awards	---

Main Cast	
Actor / Actress	**Screen Names**
Eliza Dushku	Jessie Burlingame
Desmond Harrington	Chris Flynn
Emmanuelle Chrique	Carly
Jeremy Sisto	Scott

Facts / More

Desmond Harrington broke his ankle after landing incorrectly on a log while the four of them were running from the house after awakening the killers and Emmanuelle Chrique dislocated her shoulder during the tree jump. You can hear her shoulder pop on the on the production track in the theatrical sound mix.

Unlike the sequels, there are no nudity scenes in the film. There were other versions of the script that attempted to include nude scenes, like Jessie having her clothes ripped off while tied up on the bed and Francine and Evan being killed while having sex, but none of these made it into the film.

JEEPERS CREEPERS 2	
Release Date	August 29, 2003
Budget	$17,000,000
Studio	United Artists, MGM, Myriad Pictures, American Zoetrope
Run Time	104 minutes
Sub-genre	---
Source / Inspiration	Sequel
Writers	Victor Salva

Producers	Tom Muse, Myriad Pictures, American Zoetrope
Directors	Victor Salva
Box Office	$63,100,000
Awards	---

Main Cast	
Actor / Actress	**Screen Names**
Ray Wise	Jack Taggart Sr.
Jonathan Breck	The Creeper
Eric Nenninger	Scotty Braddock
Nicki Aycox	Minxy Hayes

Facts / More

Victor Salva set the rule that the Creeper gets to eat for 23 days every 23 years, forcing a sequel to wait 23 years to be remade as the studio wouldn't like it or want it set in the future, but there was a loophole where they could set the sequel in the same 23 days as the first film.

The road scenes were all filmed on a piece of private road in California while the interior bus scenes were filmed in an airport hangar.

Meatloaf was considered for the role of the bus driver and strangely there was a point were they were considering "Like a Bat Out of Hell" for the working title. Instead they went with Jeepers Creepers 2 and used the phrase at the end of the film where the Creeper is strapped to Jack's barn wall.

HOUSE OF 1,000 CORPSES

Release Date	April 11, 2003
Budget	$7,000,000
Studio	Lions Gate Films, Goodrights
Run Time	89 minutes
Sub-genre	---
Source / Inspiration	---
Writers	Rob Zombie
Producers	Andy Gould, Goodrights
Directors	Rob Zombie
Box Office	$16,800,000
Awards	Fangoria Chainsaw Awards – Chainsaw Award
	Fantasporto – International Fantasy Film Award
	The Stinkers Bad Movie Awards – Stinkers Award

Main Cast	
Actor / Actress	**Screen Names**
Sid Haig	Captain Spulding
Karen Black	Mother Firefly

Jennifer Jostyn	Mary Knowles
Judith Drake	Skunk Ape Wife
Facts / More	

The movie was filmed in 2000, but wasn't released until 2003.

FREDDY VS JASON

Release Date	August 15, 2003
Budget	$30,000,000
Studio	New Line Cinema, Crystal Lake Entertainment
Run Time	98 minutes
Sub-genre	Slasher
Source / Inspiration	Previous franchises
Writers	Damian Shannon, Mark Swift
Producers	Sean S. Cunningham
Directors	Ronny Yu
Box Office	$116,600,000
Awards	BMI Film & TV Awards – BMI Film Music Award
	Fangoria Chainsaw Awards – Chainsaw Award

Main Cast	
Actor / Actress	**Screen Names**
Robert Englund	Freddy Krueger
Ken Kirzinger	Jason Vorhees
Monica Keena	Lori Campbell
Jason Ritter	Will Rollins
Kelly Rowland	Kia Waterson
Katharine Isabelle	Gibb
Facts / More	

The final film where Robert Englund plays Freddy Krueger.

Robert Englund reported that his make-up was so heavy he couldn't tell how hot the fires were on the sets and when he went to take his make-up off it had bonded to his face.

Robert Englund was excited at the casting of Katharine Isabelle because he was a fan of her role in the werewolf film, Ginger Snaps (2000).

Westin Hills was featured in A Nightmare on Elm Street 3: Dream Warriors.

New Line Cinema and Paramount Pictures had been working on this crossover film since the 80's, but they couldn't agree on a story.

The original concept that was developed in the 90s was Michael Myers vs Jason Vorhees, but the characters were two similar so they went with Freddy vs Jason so it was more David vs Goliath. This is also why Kane Hodder didn't get the part because he was too short and bulky.

FINAL DESTINATION 2

Release Date	January 31, 2003
Budget	$26,000,000
Studio	New Line Cinema, Zide/Perry Productions
Run Time	90 minutes
Sub-genre	---
Source / Inspiration	Sequel
Writers	J. Mackye Gruber, Eric Bress, Jeffrey Reddick
Producers	Warren Zide, Craig Perry, Zide/Perry Productions
Directors	David R. Ellis
Box Office	$90,400,000
Awards	---

Main Cast	
Actor / Actress	**Screen Names**
Ali Larter	Clear Rivers
A. J. Cook	Kimberley Corman
Michael Landis	Thomas Burke

Facts / More
The logs are CGI because they tested real logs, but they didn't bounce enough during the crash sequence.

THE TEXAS CHAINSAW MASSACRE

Release Date	October 17, 2003
Budget	$9,500,000
Studio	New Line Cinema, Next Entertainment, Platinum Dunes, Radar Pictures
Run Time	98 minutes
Sub-genre	Slasher
Source / Inspiration	Remake
Writers	Scott Kosar
Producers	Michael Bay, Mike Fleiss, Next Entertainment, Platinum Dunes, Radar Pictures
Directors	Marcus Nispel
Box Office	$107,400,000
Awards	BMI Film & TV Awards – BMI Award Key Art Awards – Key Art Award Sitges – Catalonian International Film Festival – Best Art Direction

Main Cast	
Actor / Actress	**Screen Names**
Jessica Biel	Erin
Jonathan Tucker	Morgan
Erica Leerhsen	Pepper
Mike Vogel	Andy
Eric Balfour	Kemper
Andy Bryniarski	Leatherface

Facts / More

To prepare for his role of Leatherface, Andy Bryniarski ate brisket and bread to get his weight to around 300 pounds.

This film is banned in Ukraine by the Ministry of Culture.

This is the only TCM movie where you get to see Leatherface's actual face.

2004

DAWN OF THE DEAD	
Release Date	March 19, 2004
Budget	$26,000,000
Studio	Universal Pictures, Strike Entertainment, New Amsterdam Entertainment
Run Time	100 minutes
Sub-genre	---
Source / Inspiration	Dawn of the Dead (1978) George A. Romero
Writers	James Gunn
Producers	Richard P. Rubinstein, Marc Abraham, Eric Newman, Strike Entertainment, New Amsterdam Entertainment
Directors	Zack Snyder
Box Office	$102,300,000
Awards	Golden Trailer Awards – Golden Trailer

Main Cast	
Actor / Actress	**Screen Names**
Sarah Polley	Ana
Ving Rhames	Kenneth
Jake Weber	Michael

Facts / More

Some of the camera crew would wear plastic sheets to protect them from all the fake blood flying around during gore scenes.

By the end of production, over 3,000 zombie make up effects had been created.

THE GRUDGE	
Release Date	October 22, 2004
Budget	$10,000,000
Studio	Sony Pictures, Universal Pictures, Colombia Pictures, Ghost House Pictures
Run Time	91 minutes
Sub-genre	Supernatural
Source / Inspiration	Ju-On: The Grudge (Japan)
Writers	Stephen Susco
Producers	Sam Raimi, Robert Tapert, Takashige Ichise, Colombia Pictures, Ghost House Pictures
Directors	Takashi Shimizu

Box Office	$187,200,000
Awards	BMI Film & TV Awards – BMI Film Music Award
	Fangoria Chainsaw Awards – Chainsaw Award

Main Cast	
Actor / Actress	**Screen Names**
Sarah Michelle Gellar	Karen
Jason Behr	Doug
William Mapother	Matthew

Facts / More
The crew went through a ceremony where they were blessed before filming so nothing bad happened to them.

SAW

Release Date	October 29, 2004
Budget	$1,200,000
Studio	Lions Gate Films, Twisted Pictures
Run Time	103 minutes
Sub-genre	Mystery
Source / Inspiration	Saw (Australian short film)
Writers	Leigh Whannel, James Wan
Producers	Gregg Hoffman, Oren Koules, Mark Burg, Twisted Pictures
Directors	James Wan
Box Office	$103,900,000
Awards	Brussels International Festival of Fantasy Films – Pegasus Audience Award
	Fantasporto – International Fantasy Film Award
	Golden Schmoes Awards – Golden Schmoes Award
	Gerardmer Film Festival – Special Jury Prize, Young Jury Grand Prize
	San Sebastian Horror and Fantasy Film Festival – Audience Award

Main Cast	
Actor / Actress	**Screen Names**
Leigh Whannel	Adam
Cary Elwes	Dr. Lawrence Gordon
Danny Glover	Detective David Tapp
Tobin Bell	Jigsaw

Facts / More
James Wan gambled and took no salary. Instead he took a percentage of the movie.

CLUB DREAD

Release Date	February 27, 2004
Budget	$8,600,000
Studio	Fox Searchlight Pictures, Broken Lizard Industries, Cataland Films
Run Time	103 minutes
Sub-genre	---
Source / Inspiration	---
Writers	Jay Chandrasekhar, Kevin Heffernan, Steve Lemme, Paul Soter, Erik Stolhanske
Producers	Richard Perello, Arturo Brito, Broken Lizard Industries, Cataland Films
Directors	Jay Chandrasekhar
Box Office	$7,600,000
Awards	---

Main Cast	
Actor / Actress	**Screen Names**
Elena Lyons	Stacy
Tanja Reichert	Kellie
Nat Faxon	Manny
Michael Weaver	Roy

Facts / More
The line "How many of you knew that he was circumcised and smelled like oranges?" was included in the script to make sure people were reading the script before it was green lit.

VAN HELSING

Release Date	May 7, 2004
Budget	$170,000,000
Studio	Universal Pictures, Sommers Company, Stillking Films
Run Time	131 minutes
Sub-genre	Supernatural
Source / Inspiration	Dracula (novel) by Bram Stoker, Frankenstein (novel) by Mary Shelley
Writers	Stephen Sommers
Producers	Stephen Sommers, Bob Duscay, Sommers Company, Stillking Films
Directors	Stephen Sommers
Box Office	$300,200,000
Awards	Academy of Science Fiction, Fantasy & Horror Films, USA – Saturn Award ASCAP Film & Television Music Awards – ASCAP Award

	The Stinkers Bad Movie Awards – Stinker Awad

Main Cast

Actor / Actress	Screen Names
Hugh Jackman	Van Helsing
Kate Beckinsale	Anna Valerious
Richard Roxburgh	Count Vladislaus Dracula
Josie Maran	Marishka

Facts / More

Stephen Sommers didn't want the clique werewolf that grows hair. Instead he wanted the werewolves to rip off their skin to reveal their werewolfism, executing the idea of "the beast within".

Kate Beckinsale was the last to be cast.

According to producers, the Transylvanian town was too good to pull down and was set to be the basis for a television series.

The first week's DVD sales were $65 million in North America alone, more than half the revenue from its time in theaters.

SEED OF CHUCKY

Release Date	November 11, 2004
Budget	$12,000,000
Studio	Rogue Pictures, La Sienega Productions, David Kirschner Productions
Run Time	86 minutes (R-Rated cut), 87 minutes (Unrated cut)
Sub-genre	Slasher
Source / Inspiration	Sequel
Writers	Don Mancini
Producers	David Kirschner, Corey Sienega, La Sienega Productions, David Kirschner Productions
Directors	Don Mancini
Box Office	$24,800,000
Awards	Academy of Science Fiction, Fantasy & Horror Films – Saturn Award

Main Cast

Actor / Actress	Screen Names
Brad Dourif	Chucky (voice)
Jennifer Tilly	Tiffany
Billy Boyd	Glen / Glenda
Redman	Redman

Facts / More

The is the only Chucky / Child's Play movie to date that contains nudity.

EXORCIST: THE BEGINNING

Release Date	August 20, 2004
Budget	$50,000,000
Studio	Warner Bros. Pictures, Morgan Creek Productions
Run Time	14 minutes
Sub-genre	Supernatural
Source / Inspiration	Sequel
Writers	William Wishner, Cale Carr, Alei Hawley
Producers	James G. Robinson
Directors	Renny Harlin
Box Office	$76,800,000
Awards	---

Main Cast	
Actor / Actress	**Screen Names**
Stellan Skarsgard	Father Merrin
Izabella Scorupco	Sarah
James D'Arcy	Father Francis
Remy Sweeney	Joseph

Facts / More

Liam Neeson was originally cast as Father Merrin.

William Peter Blatty stated that watching this film was his "most humiliating professional experience".

After Merrin opens the crypt there are a few frames where you see the face of a demon. The same technique was used in the original Exorcist (1973) with the "blink and you'll miss it" demon face.

Most of the film is shot in 1949.

2005

WOLF CREEK

Release Date	November 3, 2005
Budget	$1,400,000 (AU)
Studio	Roadshow Entertainment, Film Finance Corporation Australia, South Australian Film Corporation, 403 Productions, True Crime Channel, Mushroom Pictures
Run Time	99 minutes
Sub-genre	---
Source / Inspiration	The crimes of Ivan Milat (Australian Backpack Killer)
Writers	Greg McLean
Producers	David Lightfoot, Greg McLean, Film Finance Corporation Australia, South Australian Film Corporation, 403 Productions, True Crime Channel, Mushroom Pictures
Directors	Greg McLean
Box Office	$35,000,000 (AU)
Awards	Austin Fantastic Fest – Jury Prize Australian Cinematographers Society – Award of Distinction Screen Music Awards, Australia – Screen Music Awards

Main Cast	
Actor / Actress	**Screen Names**
John Jarrett	Mick Taylor
Cassandra Magrath	Liz Hunter
Kestie Morassi	Kristy Earl
Nathan Phillips	Ben Mitchell

Facts / More
The abandoned mine where they filmed had actually been the site of a real murder, but the crew weren't aware. Locals protested because they thought the film was based on those events when it was actually based on a completely different Australian killer called Ivan Milat. This is one of Quentin Taratino's favorite movies. The crater in the film is in Western Australia and is called "Wolfe Creek".

HOSTEL

Release Date	September 17, 2005 (Toronto International Film Festival), January 6, 2006
Budget	$4,800,000
Studio	Lions Gate Films, Screen Gems, Sony Pictures Releasing, Next Entertainment, Raw Nerve

Run Time	94 minutes
Sub-genre	Gore
Source / Inspiration	---
Writers	Eli Roth
Producers	Chris Briggs, Mike Fleiss, Eli Roth, Next Entertainment, Raw Nerve
Directors	Eli Roth
Box Office	$82,000,000
Awards	Austin Fantastic Fest – Jury Prize
	Empire Awards, UK – Empire Award
	Scream Awards – Scream Award

Main Cast	
Actor / Actress	**Screen Names**
Jay Hernandez	Paxton
Derek Richardson	Josh
Eythor Gudjonsson	Lio
Barbara Nedeljakova	Natalya

Facts / More

Eli Roth hired real street kids to play the BubbleGum Gang.

Staying in Room 237 is a reference to The Shining (1980).

At around 9 minutes, Quentin Tarantino appears as a shirtless German man screaming from a window.

HOUSE OF WAX

Release Date	May 6, 2005
Budget	$40,000,000
Studio	Warner Bros. Pictures, Village Roadshow Pictures, Dark Castle Entertainment
Run Time	113 minutes
Sub-genre	---
Source / Inspiration	Remake
Writers	Charles Belden, Chad Hayes, Carey W. Hayes
Producers	Joel Silver, Robert Zemeckis, Susan Levin, Village Roadshow Pictures, Dark Castle Entertainment
Directors	Jaunme Collet-Serra
Box Office	$70,100,000
Awards	Razzie Awards – Razzie Award
	Teen Choice Awards – Teen Choice Award

Main Cast	
Actor / Actress	**Screen Names**

Elisha Cuthbert	Carly Jones
Chad Michael Murray	Nick
Jared Padalecki	Wade
Paris Hilton	Paige
Brian Van Holt	Bo
Facts / More	

One of the brothers is named Vincent which is a nod to Vincent Price who appeared in House of Wa (1953).

Paris Hilton was the first actress hired and the cast was built around her.

The movie didn't make its budget back until it went to home video.

Jennifer Connelly and Kate Winslet turned down the role of Paige. Connelly chose to star in another horror film, Dark Waters (2005).

In the church where Carly hides and also in the movie theater where her and Nick hide, most of the wax figures are actual human extras wearing masks.

THE AMITYVILLE HORROR

Release Date	April 15, 2005
Budget	$19,000,000
Studio	MGM, 20th Century Fox, Dimension Films, Platinum Dunes, Radar Pictures
Run Time	89 minutes
Sub-genre	Supernatural
Source / Inspiration	The Amityville Horror (book) by Jay Anson, The Amityville Horror (1979), Ed & Lorraine Warren's investigations of the Lutz family home
Writers	Scott Kosar, Sandor Stern
Producers	Michael Bay, Andrew Form, Brad Fuller, Dimension Films, Platinum Dunes, Radar Pictures, MGM
Directors	Andrew Douglas
Box Office	$108,000,000
Awards	Golden Trailer Awards – Golden Trailer Teen Choice Awards – Teen Choice Award
Main Cast	
Actor / Actress	**Screen Names**
Ryan Reynolds	George Lutz
Melissa George	Kathy Lutz
Jesse James	Billy Lutz
Facts / More	

Megan Fox auditioned for the role of the babysitter.

The names of the Lutz children were changed to conceal their true identities, as they were in the original.

THE DEVIL'S REJECTS

Release Date	July 22, 2005
Budget	$7,000,000
Studio	Lionsgate, Tiberius Films, Cinelamda
Run Time	109 minutes
Sub-genre	---
Source / Inspiration	---
Writers	Rob Zombie
Producers	Mike Elliot, Andy Gould, Marco Mehlitz, Michael Ohoven, Rob Zombie, Cinelamda
Directors	Rob Zombie
Box Office	$20,900,000
Awards	Fangoria Chainsaw Awards – Chainsaw Award Scream Awards – Scream Award

Main Cast	
Actor / Actress	**Screen Names**
Sid Haig	Captain Spaulding
Bill Moseley	Otis
Sheri Moon Zombie	Baby
William Forsythe	Sheriff Wydell

Facts / More

Rob Zombie stated this was one of his hardest films to cut to get an R-Rating.

Las Vegas illusionist, Criss Angel, did his "Buried Alive" performance outside the Firefly ranch house with Rob Zombie as one of the spectators.

LAND OF THE DEAD

Release Date	June 24, 2005
Budget	$19,000,000
Studio	Universal Pictures, Atmosphere Entertainment MM, Romero-Grunwald Productions, Wild Bunch, Rangerkim
Run Time	97 minutes
Sub-genre	Supernatural
Source / Inspiration	---
Writers	George A. Romero
Producers	Mark Canton, Bernie Goldman, Peter Grunwald, Atmosphere Entertainment MM, Romero-Grunwald Productions, Wild Bunch, Rangerkim
Directors	George A. Romero

Box Office	$46,800,000
Awards	Fangoria Chainsaw Awards – Chainsaw Award
	Hollywood Film Awards – Hollywood Film Award

Main Cast	
Actor / Actress	**Screen Names**
Simon Baker	Riley Denbo
John Leguizamo	Cholo DeMora
Dennis Hopper	Kaufman
Asia Argento	Slack

Facts / More
George A. Romero's daughter appears in the film. She is the soldier who shoots the zombie on the electric fence.
There were four title choices before Land of the Dead... Dead City, Dead Reckoning, Twilight of the Dead and Night of the Living Dead.
This was the most expensive of Romero's zombie films.

THE EXORCISM OF EMILY ROSE

Release Date	September 9, 2005
Budget	$19,000,000
Studio	Screen Gems, Sony Pictures, Lakeshore Entertainment, Firm Films, Mist Entertainment
Run Time	121 minutes
Sub-genre	Supernatural
Source / Inspiration	---
Writers	Paul Harris Boardman, Scott Derrickson
Producers	Tom Rosenberg, Gary Lucchesi, Paul Harris Boardman, Tripp Vinson, Beau Flynn, Lakeshore Entertainment, Firm Films, Mist Entertainment
Directors	Scott Derrickson
Box Office	$145,200,000
Awards	Academy of Science Fiction, Fantasy & Horror Films, USA – Saturn Award
	Golden Trailer Awards – Golden Trailer
	MTV Movie & TV Awards – MTV Movie Award
	Scream Awards – Scream Award

Main Cast	
Actor / Actress	**Screen Names**
Jennifer Carpenter	Emily Rose
Laura Linney	Erin Burner
Tom Wilkinson	Father Moore

| Campbell Scott | Ethan Thomas |
| Colm Feore | Karl Gunderson |

Facts / More
Jennifer Carpenter's audition was so scary and convincing that she was hired on the spot.
The film makers stated they didn't want to make "just another horror film" and wanted to make a smart movie that questions whether demonic possession actually exists.

DOOM

Release Date	October 21, 2005
Budget	$70,000,000
Studio	Universal Studios, John Wells Productions, Di Bonaventura Productions
Run Time	104 minutes
Sub-genre	Video game adaptation
Source / Inspiration	Doom (Game) by id Software
Writers	Dave Callaham, Wesley Strick
Producers	Lorenzo Di Bonaventura, John Wells Productions, Di Bonaventura Productions
Directors	Andrzej Bartkowiak
Box Office	$58,700,000
Awards	---

Main Cast	
Actor / Actress	**Screen Names**
Dwayne "The Rock" Johnson	Sarge
Karl Urban	John Grimm
Rosamund Pike	Samantha Grimm
Deobia Oparei	Destroyer
Ben Daniels	Goat
Richard Brake	Portman

Facts / More
The Rock was offered the role of John Grimm, but took the role of Sarge instead.
The FPS sequence that pays tribute to the video game took two weeks to shoot.
Vin Diesel turned down the lead role.

THE DESCENT

Release Date	July 8, 2005 (UK), August 4, 2006
Budget	£3,500,000
Studio	Pathe Distribution, Celador Films, Northmen Productions

Run Time	100 minutes
Sub-genre	---
Source / Inspiration	---
Writers	Neil Marshall
Producers	Christian Colson, Celador Films, Northmen Productions
Directors	Neil Marshall
Box Office	$57,100,000
Awards	Academy of Science Fiction, Fantasy & Horror Films, USA – Saturn Award
	British Independent Film Awards – British Independent Film Award
	Empire Awards, UK – Empire Award
	Evening Standard British Film Awards – Evening Standard British Film Award
	Golden Schmoes Awards – Golden Schmoes Award
	Golden Trailer Awards – Golden Trailer
	Philadelphia Film Festival

Main Cast	
Actor / Actress	**Screen Names**
Shauna MacDonald	Sarah
Natalie Mendoza	Juno
Alex Reid	Beth
Saskia Mulder	Rebecca

Facts / More
The film makers felt it was too dangerous to film in a real cave so they decided to build their own for shooting. No real caves appear anywhere in the film.
Neil Marshall kept the crawler separate from the women so when they saw the crawler it was for the first time. They went screaming and running so the technique definitely worked.

HARD CANDY

Release Date	January 21, 2005 (Sundance), April 14, 2006
Budget	$950,000
Studio	Lionsgate, Vulcan Productions, Launchpad Productions
Run Time	104 minutes
Sub-genre	---
Source / Inspiration	---
Writers	Brian Nelson
Producers	Rosanne Korenberg, Paul Allen, Vulcan Productions, Launchpad Productions
Directors	David Slade

Box Office	$8,300,000
Awards	Austin Film Critic's Association – AFCA Award
	Malaga International Week of Fantastic Cinema – Best Actress, Best Cinematography, Best Director, Youth Jury Award
	Phoenix Film Critics Society Awards – PFCS Award
	Sitges – Catalonian International Film Festival – Audience Award, Best Film, Best Screenplay
	Women Film Critics Circle Awards – WFCC Award

Main Cast	
Actor / Actress	**Screen Names**
Patrick Wilson	Jeff Kohlver
Elliot Page	Hayley Stark

Facts / More
Filmed in 18 days.

DOMINION: PREQUEL TO THE EXORCIST

Release Date	May 20, 2005
Budget	$30,000,000
Studio	Warner Bros. Pictures, Morgan Creek Productions
Run Time	116 minutes
Sub-genre	Supernatural
Source / Inspiration	Sequel (Prequel)
Writers	William Wisher, Caleb Carr
Producers	James G. Robinson
Directors	Paul Schrader
Box Office	$251,495
Awards	---

Main Cast	
Actor / Actress	**Screen Names**
Stellan Skarsgard	Father Lankester Merrin
Gabriel Mann	Father Francis
Billy Crawford	Cheche

Facts / More
Liam Neeson was originally cast as Father Merrin.

THE DARK

Release Date	May, 2005
Budget	---
Studio	Miramax Films, Constantin Films
Run Time	93 minutes
Sub-genre	Supernatural
Source / Inspiration	Sheep (novel) by Simon Maginn
Writers	Stephen Massicotte
Producers	Paul W. S. Anderson, Jeremy Bolt, Steve Christian, Robert Kulzer, Constantin Films
Directors	John Fawcett
Box Office	---
Awards	---

Main Cast	
Actor / Actress	**Screen Names**
Maria Bello	Adelle
Sean Bean	James
Sophie Stuckley	Sarah

Facts / More
This is one of the few films Sean Bean stars in where he doesn't die.

2006

THE HILLS HAVE EYES

Release Date	March 10, 2006
Budget	15,000,000
Studio	Fox Searchlight Pictures, Major Studio Partners, Craven/Maddalena Films
Run Time	106 minutes
Sub-genre	---
Source / Inspiration	Remake
Writers	Alexandre Aja, Gregory Levasseur
Producers	Wes Craven, Marianne Maddalena, Peter Locke, Major Studio Partners, Craven/Maddalena Films
Directors	Alexandre Aja
Box Office	$70,000,000
Awards	Fangoria Chainsaw Awards – Chainsaw Award

Main Cast	
Actor / Actress	**Screen Names**
Michael Bailey Smith	Pluto
Ted Levine	Big Bob
Kathleen Quinlan	Ethel
Dan Byrd	Bobby

Facts / More
Almost all of Ted Levine's actions and lines were improvised.
This was filmed in Morocco and over 16 different nationalities worked on it. Sand storms occurred on a daily basis.

WHEN A STRANGER CALLS

Release Date	February 3, 2006
Budget	$15,000,000
Studio	Sony Pictures, TeleStranger Productions
Run Time	87 minutes
Sub-genre	---
Source / Inspiration	Remake
Writers	Jake Wade Wall
Producers	John Davis, Wyck Godfrey, Ken Lemberger

Directors	Simon West
Box Office	$67,100,000
Awards	---

Main Cast	
Actor / Actress	**Screen Names**
Camilla Belle	Jill Johnson
Tommy Flanagan	Stranger

Facts / More

Camille Belle had to be convinced to take the role because she didn't want to star in a horror movie. When she was told they were going for a psychological thriller she took the role and abandoned the opportunity to star in Black Christmas (2006).

The scar on Tommy Flanagan's face that's shown at the end when he's taken away is actually a real scar.

Jill doesn't get calls or stalked until nearly an hour into the movie.

PULSE

Release Date	August 11, 2006
Budget	$20,500,000
Studio	The Weinstein Company, Dimension Films, Distant Horizon
Run Time	86 minutes
Sub-genre	---
Source / Inspiration	Remake (Japan)
Writers	Wes Craven, Ray Wright
Producers	Anant Singh, Brian Cox, Michael Leahy, Joel Soisson, Distant Horizon
Directors	Jim Sonzero
Box Office	$30,000,000
Awards	---

Main Cast	
Actor / Actress	**Screen Names**
Kristen Bell	Mattie
Ian Somerholder	Dexter
Christina Milian	Isabella Fuentes
Rick Gonzales	Stone

Facts / More

The trailer features footage from the original Japanese film (Pulse 2001).

Another film, also titled Pulse, from 1988 isn't linked to this film despite a similar plot of supernaturally-charged electrical entities.

THE OMEN

Release Date	June 6, 2006
Budget	$25,000,000
Studio	20th Century Fox
Run Time	110 minutes
Sub-genre	Supernatural
Source / Inspiration	---
Writers	David Seltzer
Producers	Glenn Williamson, John Moore
Directors	John Moore
Box Office	$120,000,000
Awards	Fangoria Chainsaw Awards – Chainsaw Award

Main Cast	
Actor / Actress	**Screen Names**
Predrag Bjelac	Vatacan Observatory Priest
Seamus Davey-Fitzpatrick	Damien
Liev Schreiber	Pope

Facts / More
In digits, the release date of this film was 6-6-06 which is also the 30th anniversary of the originaL

THE TEXAS CHAINSAW MASSACRE: THE BEGINNING

Release Date	October 6, 2006
Budget	$16,000,000
Studio	New Line Cinema, Next Entertainment, Platinum Dunes
Run Time	91 minutes
Sub-genre	Slasher
Source / Inspiration	Remake
Writers	Sheldon Turner, David J. Schow
Producers	Michael Bay, Mike Fleiss, Tobe Hooper, Kim Henkel, Andrew Form, Brad Fuller, Next Entertainment, Platinum Dunes
Directors	Jonathan Liebesman
Box Office	$51,800,000
Awards	---

Main Cast	
Actor / Actress	**Screen Names**
Jordana Brewster	Chrissie
Taylor Handley	Dean

Diora Baird	Bailey
Matt Bomer	Eric
Andrew Bryniarski	Leatherface / Thomas Hewitt
Facts / More	

Jordana Brewster and Andrew Form met on the set, starting dating and then ultimately got married and had their first child in 2013.

Bailey's throat-slitting scene was shot nine times with slight variations each time.

SLITHER

Release Date	March 31, 2006
Budget	$15,000,000
Studio	Universal Pictures, Brightlight Pictures, Gold Circle Films, Strike Entertainment
Run Time	95 minutes
Sub-genre	---
Source / Inspiration	---
Writers	James Gunn
Producers	Paul Brooks, Eric Newman, Brightlight Pictures, Gold Circle Films, Strike Entertainment
Directors	James Gunn
Box Office	$12,800,000
Awards	Academy of Science Fiction, Fantasy & Horror Films, USA – Saturn Award
	Fangoria Chainsaw Awards – Chainsaw Award

Main Cast	
Actor / Actress	**Screen Names**
Nathan Fillion	Bill Pardy
Don Thompson	Wally
Gregg Henry	Jack MacReady
Elizabeth Banks	Starla Grant
Facts / More	

James Gunn said that he is a veteran of gore effects, but the dog corpse that Starla finds in the basement made him sick.

SILENT HILL

Release Date	April 21, 2006
Budget	$50,000,000
Studio	Alliance Atlantis, Metropolitan Film Export, Davis Films, Konami, Silent Hill DCP, Inc.
Run Time	125 minutes

Sub-genre	---
Source / Inspiration	Centralia, Pennsylvania, USA (abandoned mining town)
Writers	Roger Avary
Producers	Samuel Hadida, Don Carmody, Davis Films, Konami, Silent Hill DCP, Inc.
Directors	Christophe Gans
Box Office	$100,600,000
Awards	---

Main Cast	
Actor / Actress	**Screen Names**
Radha Mitchell	Rose Da Silva
Sean Bean	Christopher De Silva
Laurie Holden	Cybil Bennett
Deborah Kara Unger	Dahlia Gillespie

Facts / More
Many of the creatures in the film were played by dancers so they were more flexible and could make the disturbing movements. Centralia in Pennsylvania served as the inspiration for both the video game and the movie. It's an abandoned mining town where a fire still burns under the surface.

BLACK CHRISTMAS

Release Date	December 25, 2006
Budget	$9,000,000
Studio	Dimension Films, MGM, 2929 Productions, Adelstein-Parouse Productions, Hard Eight Pictures, Hoban Segal Productions
Run Time	84 minutes (European cut), 90 minutes (North American cut)
Sub-genre	Christmas
Source / Inspiration	Black Christmas (1974) film
Writers	Glen Morgan, Roy Moore
Producers	Marty Adelstein, Dawn Parouse, Victor Solnicki, Steve Hoban, James Wong, Glen Morgan, 2929 Productions, Adelstein-Parouse Productions, Hard Eight Pictures, Hoban Segal Productions
Directors	Glen Morgan
Box Office	$21,500,000
Awards	---

Main Cast	
Actor / Actress	**Screen Names**
Katie Cassidy	Kelli Presley (Katie Cassidy)

Facts / More
Filmed in Canada and not screened for critics before its release.

2007

HALLOWEEN

Release Date	August 31, 2007
Budget	15,000,000
Studio	The Weinstein Company, Dimension Films, MGM, Nightfall Productions, Spectacle Entertainment Group, Trancas International
Run Time	110 minutes
Sub-genre	Slasher
Source / Inspiration	Remake
Writers	Rob Zombie
Producers	Malek Akkad, Andy Gould, Rob Zombie, Dimension Films, Nightfall Productions, Spectacle Entertainment Group, Trancas International
Directors	Rob Zombie
Box Office	$80,400,000
Awards	Academy of Science Fiction, Fantasy & Horror Films, USA – Saturn Award Rondo Hatton Classic Horror Awards – Rondo Statuette Scream Awards – Scream Award

Main Cast

Actor / Actress	Screen Names
Tyler Mane	Michael Myers
Malcolm McDowell	Dr. Sam Loomis
Sheri Moon Zombie	Deborah Myers

Facts / More

Tyler Mane is the tallest actor to play Michael Myers at 6'8. This is also the longest Halloween film at 121 minutes.

This is the first Halloween movie where Michael Myers talks.

VACANCY

Release Date	April 20, 2007
Budget	$19,000,000
Studio	Sony Pictures, Screen Gems, Hal Lieberman Company
Run Time	85 minutes
Sub-genre	---
Source / Inspiration	---

Writers	Mark L. Smith
Producers	Hal Lieberman
Directors	Nimrod Antal
Box Office	$35,300,000
Awards	Scream Awards – Scream Award

Main Cast	
Actor / Actress	**Screen Names**
Luke Wilson	David Fox
Kate Beckinsale	Amy Fox
Frank Whaley	Mason

Facts / More

The advertising strategy for the film made use of the Internet as well as a toll-free phone number. The number was made to sound as if one is actually calling the Pinewood Motel. In the background, screaming can be heard accompanying the voice of the proprietor, who informs callers about "slashing" prices and the "killer" deals that the motel has, if it has a vacancy. The voice of the proprietor is none other than Frank Whaley's. The toll free phone number for the ad was 1-888-9-VACANCY (1-888-982-22629). The toll-free phone number is no longer valid.

The snuff films that play were filmed on the first day of shooting. The complete snuff films are listed on the film's home video release.

In the end, when the BMW is crashed into the motel, this was a practical effect that damaged the set. It wasn't computer generated effects.

TRICK 'R TREAT

Release Date	December 9, 2007 (Butt-Numb-A-Thon), October 6, 2009
Budget	$12,000,000
Studio	Warner Bros. Pictures, Warner Premiere, Legendary Pictures, Bad Hat Harry Productions
Run Time	82 minutes
Sub-genre	---
Source / Inspiration	---
Writers	Michael Dougherty
Producers	Bryan Singer, Warner Bros. Pictures, Warner Premiere, Legendary Pictures, Bad Hat Harry Productions
Directors	Michael Dougherty
Box Office	---
Awards	Fangoria Chainsaw Awards – Chainsaw Award
	Fright Meter Awards – Fright Meter Award
	Screamfest – Audience Award

Main Cast	
Actor / Actress	**Screen Names**

| Dylan Baker | Steven |
| Rochelle Aytes | Maria |

Facts / More
The werewolf transformation is said to be a nod at The Howling (1981).

ZODIAC

Release Date	March 2, 2007
Budget	$85,000,000
Studio	Paramount Pictures, Warner Bros. Pictures, Phoenix Pictures
Run Time	157 minutes
Sub-genre	True Crime
Source / Inspiration	Zodiac Killer
Writers	James Vanderbilt
Producers	Mike Medavoy, Arnold W. Messer, Bradley J. Fischer, James Vanderbilt, Cean Chaffin, Phoenix Pictures
Directors	David Fincher
Box Office	$84,700,000
Awards	Dublin Film Critics Circle Awards – DFCC Faro Island Film Festival – Golden Train Award Il Festival Nazionale del Doppiaggio Voci nell'Ombra – Film Award International Film Music Critics Award - IFMCA

Main Cast	
Actor / Actress	**Screen Names**
Jake Gyllenhaal	Robert Graysmith
Mark Ruffalo	Inspector David Toschi
Robert Downey Jr.	Paul Avery

Facts / More
Based on the real-life Zodiac killer who taunted San Fransisco authorities and newspapers. The case remains unsolved. Lake Berryessa was the filming location and the real life murder location. Fincher had trees flown in by helicopter because the area had changed since the murder in 1969 and he wanted the location to be as accurate as possible. The film was edited using Final Cut Pro.

PARANORMAL ACTIVITY

Release Date	October 14, 2007 (Screamfest), September 25, 2009
Budget	$15,000 (post production = $215,000)

Studio	Paramount Pictures, Blumhouse Productions
Run Time	86 minutes
Sub-genre	Supernatural / Found Footage
Source / Inspiration	---
Writers	Oren Peli
Producers	Jason Blum, Oren Peli, Steven Schneider
Directors	Oren Peli
Box Office	$193,400,000
Awards	Screamfest – Festival Trophy, Honorable Mention Teen Choice Awards – Teen Choice Award

Main Cast	
Actor / Actress	**Screen Names**
Katie Featherstone	Katie
Micah Sloat	Micah

Facts / More
This was Paramount's second biggest ROI. They acquires the U.S rights for $350,000, while the film made $193 million. The first film that gave Paramount the biggest return on investment was The Blair Witch Project.
All the effects were practical and done in-camera. Oren Peli shot the entire film in his own home and bought the Ouija board from Costco.

HANNIBAL RISING

Release Date	February 9, 2007
Budget	$50,000,000
Studio	Quinta Communications, Momentum Pictures, SPI International, Filmauro, The Weinstein Company, MGM, Dino De Laurentiis Company, Carthago Films, Zephyr Films, Etic Films
Run Time	121 minutes
Sub-genre	---
Source / Inspiration	Sequel
Writers	Thomas Harris
Producers	Dino De Laurentiis, Martha De Laurentiis, Tarak Ben Ammar, Dino De Laurentiis Company, Carthago Films, Zephyr Films, Etic Films
Directors	Peter Webber
Box Office	$82,200,000
Awards	---

Main Cast	
Actor / Actress	**Screen Names**
Gaspard Ulliel	Hannibal Lecter
Gong Li	Lady Murasaki

Richard Leaf	Father Lecter

Facts / More
It's seen in this film that the young Hannibal Lecter is left handed, but in the rest of the saga, Sir Anthony Hopkins is right handed.

DEAD SILENCE

Release Date	March 16, 2007
Budget	$20,000,000
Studio	Universal Pictures, Twisted Pictures
Run Time	89 minutes, 92 minutes (Unrated cut)
Sub-genre	Supernatural
Source / Inspiration	---
Writers	Leigh Whannell, James Wan,
Producers	Gregg Hoffman, Oren Koules, Mark Burg, Twisted Pictures
Directors	James Wan
Box Office	$22,400,000
Awards	---

Main Cast	
Actor / Actress	**Screen Names**
Ryan Kwanten	Jamie Ashen
Amber Valletta	Ella Ashen
Donnie Wahlberg	Det. Lipton

Facts / More
Due to the film's box office flop, the plans for a sequel were scrapped.
The film was made into a horror house at Universal's Halloween Horror Nights in 2007.

1408

Release Date	June 22, 2007
Budget	$25,000,000
Studio	The Weinstein Company, MGM, Dimension Films, Di Bonaventura Pictures
Run Time	104 minutes
Sub-genre	---
Source / Inspiration	---
Writers	Matt Greenberg, Scott Alexander, Larry Karaszewski
Producers	Lorenzo Di Bonaventura, Dimension Films, Di Bonaventura Pictures
Directors	Mikael Hafstrom

Box Office	$133,000,000
Awards	ASCAP Film & Television Music Awards – ASCAP Award
	Fajr Film Festival – Audience Award
	Fright Meter Awards – Fright Meter Award
	Young Artist Awads – Young Artist Award

Main Cast	
Actor / Actress	**Screen Names**
John Cusack	Mike Enslin
Tony Shalhoub	Sam Farrell
Len Cariou	Mike's Father

Facts / More
The Emily Morgan Hotel in San Antonio, Texas have sealed off room 1408 due to alleged paranormal activity.

HOSTEL 2

Release Date	June 8, 2007
Budget	$10,200,000
Studio	Lionsgate, Screen Gems, Sony Pictures, Next Entertainment, Raw Nerve
Run Time	94 minutes
Sub-genre	Torture
Source / Inspiration	Sequel
Writers	Eli Roth
Producers	Chris Briggs, Mike Fleiss, Eli Roth, Next Entertainment, Raw Nerve
Directors	Eli Roth
Box Office	$35,600,000
Awards	---

Main Cast	
Actor / Actress	**Screen Names**
Lauren German	Beth
Roger Bart	Stuart
Heather Matarazzo	Lorna

Facts / More
The film recouped triple its budget in its theatrical release. Together, both Hostel films cost $15,000,000 to make and grossed a total of $115,000,000.
During the check-in scene, you can see Pulp Fiction (1994) playing on the television in the background.

THE POUGHKEEPSIE TAPES

Release Date	October 10, 2017
Budget	---
Studio	MGM, Orion Pictures
Run Time	86 minutes
Sub-genre	Found Footage
Source / Inspiration	---
Writers	Drew Dowdle, John Erick Dowdle
Producers	Drew Dowdle
Directors	John Erick Dowdle
Box Office	---
Awards	---

Main Cast	
Actor / Actress	**Screen Names**
Stacy Chbosky	Cheryl Dempsey
Ben Messmer	Edward Carver
Samantha Robson	Samantha

Facts / More
Shot in just 15 days.
Despite mixed reviews, this film has a small cult following. Fans were eager for the movie to get a Blu-ray release, which it finally got in October 2017.

30 DAYS OF NIGHT

Release Date	October 19, 2007
Budget	$30,000,000
Studio	Sony Pictures, Colombia Pictures, Dark Horse Entertainment, Ghost House Pictures
Run Time	14 minutes
Sub-genre	---
Source / Inspiration	30 Days of Night (Comic book) by Steve Niles
Writers	Steve Niles, Stuart Beattie, Brian Nelson
Producers	Sam Raimi, Robert Tapert, Colombia Pictures, Dark Horse Entertainment, Ghost House Pictures
Directors	David Slade
Box Office	$75,500,000
Awards	---

Main Cast	
Actor / Actress	**Screen Names**

Josh Hartnett	Eben Oleson
Melissa George	Stella Oleson
Danny Hustan	Marlow
Ben Foster	The Stranger
Facts / More	

The language the vampires speak is a completely new language and was created just for the film with theh help of a linguistics professor from a New Zealand university. The film was also shot in New Zealand.

All of the vampires have named, but they're not listed until the end credits.

THE STRANGERS

Release Date	May 30, 2008
Budget	$9,000,000
Studio	Universal Pictures, Rogue Pictures, Vertigo Entertainment, Mandate Pictures, Intrepid Pictures
Run Time	85 minutes
Sub-genre	True Crime
Source / Inspiration	Real-life Manson family / Tate murders
Writers	Bryan Bertino
Producers	Doug Davison, Roy Lee, Nathan Kahane, Rogue Pictures, Vertigo Entertainment, Mandate Pictures, Intrepid Pictures
Directors	Bryan Bertino
Box Office	$82,400,000
Awards	Scream Awards – Scream Award

Main Cast

Actor / Actress	Screen Names
Scott Speedman	James Hoyt
Liv Tyler	Kristen McKay
Gemma Ward	Dollface

Facts / More

Thee entire film was shot with hand-held cameras or steady cams.

Th exterior of the house was shot at a real farm house, but the interior was built on a sound stage.

This film is arguably based on the Keddie Murders from 1981 in California, but no one connected with the film has supported this argument. Another film called Cabin 28 (2017) was directly based on them. The Keddie murders are still unsolved.

PROM NIGHT

Release Date	April 11, 2008
Budget	$20,000,000
Studio	Screen Gems, Sony Pictures, Prom Productions
Run Time	88 minutes
Sub-genre	---
Source / Inspiration	Remake
Writers	J. S. Cardone

Producers	Neal H. Moritz, Toby Jaffe, Prom Productions
Directors	Nelson McCormick
Box Office	$57,200,000
Awards	Fangoria Chainsaw Awards – Chainsaw Award

Main Cast	
Actor / Actress	**Screen Names**
Brittany Snow	Donna Keppel
Scott Porter	Bobby
Jessica Stroup	Claire
Dana Davis	Lisa Hines

Facts / More
During the scene at the salon, the original Myers house from Halloween (1978) can be sen out the window. Jamie Lee Curtis also starred in the original Prom Night (1980).

MIDNIGHT MEAT TRAIN

Release Date	August 1, 2008
Budget	$15,000,000
Studio	Lionsgate, Lake Shore Entertainment, Midnight Picture Show, Greenestreet Films
Run Time	98 minutes
Sub-genre	Slasher
Source / Inspiration	The Midnight Meat Train (Horror book series) by Clive Barker
Writers	Jeff Buhler
Producers	Clive Barker, Jorge Saralegui, Eric Reid, Richard Wright, Tom Rosenberg, Gary Lucchesi, Lionsgate, Lake Shore Entertainment, Midnight Picture Show, Greenestreet Films
Directors	Ryuhei Kitamura
Box Office	$3,500,000
Awards	Gerard Film Festival – Audience Award, SCI FI Jury Award

Main Cast	
Actor / Actress	**Screen Names**
Bradley Cooper	Leon
Vinnie Jones	Mahogany
Leslie Bibb	Maya
Brooke Shields	Susan Hoff

Facts / More
This film as originally meant to be a sequel to Candyman (1992), it was originally written by Clive Barker in 1984.
The three main cast are members of the MCU. Bradley Cooper doe the voice of Rocket Racoon, Leslie Bibb plays Christine Everheart in Iron Man (2008) and Iron Man 2 (2010), and Vinnie Jones plays Cain Marko AKA Juggernaut in -Men 3: The Last Stand.

MIRRORS

Release Date	August 15, 2008
Budget	$35,000,000
Studio	20th Century Fox, Regency Enterprises, New Regency
Run Time	111 minutes
Sub-genre	---
Source / Inspiration	Into the Mirror (South Korean horror film)
Writers	Alexandre Aja, Greggory Levasseur
Producers	Alexander Milchan, Gregory Levasseur, Regency Enterprises, New Regency
Directors	Aleandre Aja
Box Office	$78,100,000
Awards	---

Main Cast

Actor / Actress	Screen Names
Kiefer Sutherland	Ben Carson
Paula Patton	Amy Carson
Cameron Boyce	Michael Carson

Facts / More

Anna is the name of the first possessed girl. Spelled backwards, as it would appear in a mirror, it's the same.

FRIDAY THE 13TH

Release Date	February 13, 2009
Budget	$19,000,000
Studio	Warner Bros. Pictures, Paramount Pictures, New Line Cinema, Platinum Dunes, Crystal Lake Entertainment
Run Time	97 minutes
Sub-genre	Slasher
Source / Inspiration	Remake
Writers	Damian Shannon, Mark Swift, Mark Wheaton,
Producers	Ean S. Cunningham, Michael Bay, Andrew Form, Brad Fuller, Paramount Pictures, New Line Cinema, Platinum Dunes, Crystal Lake Entertainment
Directors	Marcus Nispel
Box Office	$92,700,000
Awards	Fangoria Chainsaw Awards – Chainsaw Award
	Teen Choice Awards – Teen Choice Award

Main Cast	
Actor / Actress	**Screen Names**
Derek Mears	Jason Voorhees
Jared Padalecki	Clay Miller
Danielle Panabaker	Jenna
Amaanda Righetti	Whitney Miller

Facts / More

Including this film, Jason has killed around 200 people in the total franchise.

This film has one of the longest prologues in horror film history. The title card doesn't play until 25 minutes into the film.

The film was released on Friday the 13th.

JENNIFER'S BODY

Release Date	September 18, 2009
Budget	$16,000,000
Studio	20th Century Fox, Fox Atomic, Dune Entertainment
Run Time	102 minutes
Sub-genre	---

Source / Inspiration	---
Writers	Diablo Cody
Producers	Daniel Dubiecki, Mason Novick, Jason Reitman, Fox Atomic, Dune Entertainment
Directors	Karyn Kusama
Box Office	$31,600,000
Awards	MTV Movie & TV Awards – MTV Movie Award Teen Choice Awards – Teen Choice Award Yoga Awards – Yoga Award

Main Cast	
Actor / Actress	**Screen Names**
Megan Fox	Jennifer
Amanda Seyfried	Needy
Johnny Simmons	Chip Dove

Facts / More
Megan Fox and Amanda Seyfried have said that this is their favorite film they've each starred in.
Hershey's Chocolate Syrup was used for Jennifer's black vomit scene, along with the help of some CGI.

THE LAST HOUSE ON THE LEFT

Release Date	March 13, 2009
Budget	$15,000,000
Studio	Universal Pictures, Rogue Pictures, Midnight Entertainment, Crystal Lake Entertainment, Scion Films, Amber Entertainment, Craven-Maddalena, Cunningham Productions
Run Time	110 minutes
Sub-genre	---
Source / Inspiration	Remake
Writers	Adam Alleca, Carl Ellsworth
Producers	Wes Craven, Sean S. Cunningham, Marianne Maddalena, Rogue Pictures, Midnight Entertainment, Crystal Lake Entertainment, Scion Films, Amber Entertainment, Craven-Maddalena, Cunningham Productions
Directors	Dennis Iliadis
Box Office	$45,200,000
Awards	BIFFF – Silver Raven

Main Cast	
Actor / Actress	**Screen Names**
Garret Dillahunt	Krug
Michael Bowen	Morton
Josh Coxx	Giles

Riki Lindhome	Sadie
Aaron Paul	Francis
Sara Paxton	Mari

Facts / More
In the motel room scene, you can see bruises on Paige and Mari's legs. This is because they did their own stunts during the forest scene and the bruises were too severe to cover up with make up.
In an interview, Sara Paxton shared that the rape scene took 17 hours to film.

HALLOWEEN II

Release Date	August 28, 2009
Budget	$15,000,000
Studio	Dimension Films, The Weinstein Company, Spectacle Entertainment Group, Trancas International Films
Run Time	105 minutes
Sub-genre	Slasher
Source / Inspiration	Remake / Sequel
Writers	Rob Zombie
Producers	Malek Akkad, Andy Gould, Rob Zombie, Dimension Films, Spectacle Entertainment Group, Trancas International Films
Directors	Rob Zombie
Box Office	$39,400,000
Awards	Academy of Science Fiction, Fantasy & Horror Films, USA – Saturn Award

Main Cast	
Actor / Actress	**Screen Names**
Tyler Mane	Michael Myers
Sheri Moon Zombie	Deborah Myers
Malcolm McDowell	Dr. Sam Loomis

Facts / More
John Carpenter was offered a cameo in the film by Rob Zombie, but he declined.
This is the first Halloween movie where Michael Myers walks around without a mask on.

ORPHAN

Release Date	July 24, 2009
Budget	$20,000,000
Studio	Warner Bros. Pictures, Kinowelt Filmverleih, Dark Castle Entertainment, Appian Way Productions, Studio Babelberg Motion Pictures, Studio Canal
Run Time	123 minutes

Sub-genre	Mystery
Source / Inspiration	---
Writers	David Lesie Johnson-McGoldrick, Alex Mace
Producers	Joel Silver, Susan Downey, Leonardo DiCaprio, Jennifer Davison Killoran, Dark Castle Entertainment, Appian Way Productions, Studio Babelberg Motion Pictures, Studio Canal
Directors	Jaume Collet-Serra
Box Office	$78,800,000
Awards	Fright Meter Awards – Fright Meter Award

Main Cast	
Actor / Actress	**Screen Names**
Vera Farmiga	Kate
Peter Sarsgaard	John
Isabelle Fuhrman	Esther
Jimmy Bennett	Max

Facts / More

The seduction scene between Esther and John was originally written to be more sexual and graphic, but much of the content and dialogue was cut from the film.

The film was shipped to theaters under the code name "Infant Terror".

THE STEPFATHER

Release Date	October 16, 2009
Budget	$20,000,000
Studio	Sony Pictures, Screen Gems
Run Time	101 minutes
Sub-genre	---
Source / Inspiration	Remake
Writers	J. S. Cardone, Donald E. Westlake, Carolyn Lefcourt, Brian Garfield
Producers	Mark Morgan, Greg Moordian, Screen Gems
Directors	Nelson McMormick
Box Office	$31,200,000
Awards	---

Main Cast	
Actor / Actress	**Screen Names**
Dylan Walsh	David Harris / Grady Edwards
Sela Ward	Susan Harding
Penn Badgley	Ichael Harding
Amber Heard	Kelly Porter

<table>
<tr><td colspan="2" align="center">Facts / More</td></tr>
<tr><td colspan="2">The 19787 R-Rated film had a teenage step-daughter with a nude scene during a shower, but the PG-13 remake changed it to a step-son with no nudity.</td></tr>
</table>

MY BLOODY VALENTINE

Release Date	January 16, 2009
Budget	$14,000,000
Studio	Lionsgate
Run Time	101 minutes
Sub-genre	Slasher
Source / Inspiration	Remake
Writers	Todd Farmer, Zane Smith
Producers	Jack Murray, Lionsgate
Directors	Patrick Lussier
Box Office	$100,700,000
Awards	---

Main Cast	
Actor / Actress	**Screen Names**
Jensen Ackles	Tom Hanniger
Jaime King	Sarah Palmer
Kerr Smith	Axel Palmer
Betsy Rue	Irene

Facts / More
A flyer on the wall indicates that Valentine's Day was Saturday 14th, which would mean the previous day was Friday the 13th.
The film was made into a haunted house at Universal's "Halloween Horror Nights".
Jensen Ackles wears the same jacket in the Supernatural series.

DRAG ME TO HELL

Release Date	May 29,2009
Budget	$30,000,000
Studio	Universal Pictures, Ghost House Pictures
Run Time	99 minutes
Sub-genre	Supernatural
Source / Inspiration	---
Writers	Sam Raimi, Ivan Raimi

Producers	Robert Tapert, Grant Curtis, Ghost House Productions
Directors	Sam Raimi
Box Office	$90,800,000
Awards	Academy of Science Fiction, Fantasy & Horror Films – Saturn Award
	Fangoria Chainsaw Awards – Chainsaw Award
	International Film Music Critics Awards – IFMCA
	Scream Awards – Scream Award

Main Cast	
Actor / Actress	**Screen Names**
Alison Lohman	Christine Brown
Justin Long	Clay Dalton
Lorna Raver	Mrs. Ganush
Dileep Rao	Rham Jas

Facts / More
The yellow Delta '88 is the same car used in the Evil Dead films.

THE HAUNTING IN CONNECTICUT

Release Date	March 27, 2009
Budget	$10,000,000
Studio	Lionsgate, Gold Circle Films, Integrated Films
Run Time	102 minutes
Sub-genre	Supernatural
Source / Inspiration	Ed & Lorraine Warren paranormal investigations
Writers	Adam Simon, Tim Metcalfe
Producers	Paul Brooks, Andrew Trapini, Daniel Farrands, Wendy Rhoads, Gold Circle Films, Integrated Films
Directors	Peter Cornwell
Box Office	$77,000,000
Awards	Young Artist Awards – Young Artist Award

Main Cast	
Actor / Actress	**Screen Names**
Virginia Madsen	Sara Campbell
Kyle Gallner	Matt Campbell
Amanda Crew	Wendy

Facts / More
The movie is based on the real-life stories of Al and Carmen Snedeker who lived in a reportedly haunted house in Southington, Connecticut

INSIDIOUS

Release Date	September 14, 2010 (TIFF), April 1, 2011
Budget	$1,500,000
Studio	FilmDistrict, Sony Pictures, Haunted Movies, Stage 6 Films, Alliance Films, IM Global
Run Time	101 minutes
Sub-genre	Supernatural
Source / Inspiration	---
Writers	Leigh Whannel
Producers	Jason Blum, Steven Schneider, Oren Peli, Haunted Movies, Stage 6 Films, Alliance Films, IM Global
Directors	James Wan
Box Office	$99,500,000
Awards	Fangoria Chainsaw Awards – Chainsaw Award
	Fright Meter Awards – Fright Meter Award
	IGN Summer Movie Awards – IGN People's Choice Award
	Neuchatel International Fantastic Film Festival – Titra Film Award

Main Cast

Actor / Actress	Screen Names
Patrick Wilson	Josh Lambert
Rose Byrne	Renai Lambert
Ty Simpkins	Dalton Lambert
Lin Shaye	Elise Rainier

Facts / More

The film was shot in just three weeks.

Although the old demonic woman was played by a man, it wasn't until the sequel that film makers actually decided it was a man dressed as a woman.

A NIGHTMARE ON ELM STREET

Release Date	April 30, 2010
Budget	$35,000,000
Studio	Warner Bros. Pictures, New Line Cinema, Platinum Dunes
Run Time	90 minutes
Sub-genre	Slasher

Source / Inspiration	Remake
Writers	Wesley Strick, Eric Heisserer
Producers	Michael Bay, Andrew Form, Brad Fuller, New Line Cinema, Platinum Dunes
Directors	Samuel Bayer
Box Office	$115,600,000
Awards	Fangoria Chainsaw Awards – Chainsaw Award
	People's Choice Awards, USA – People's Choice Award

Main Cast	
Actor / Actress	**Screen Names**
Jackie Earl Haley	Freddy Krueger
Rooney Mara	Nancy Holbrook
Kyle Gallner	Quentin Smith

Facts / More

Freddy's red and green seater was knitted by Judy Graham, the same woman who knitted the Freddy's sweater in the original A Nightmare on Elm Street (1984).

Although Jackie Haley decided to accept the role and was excited about it, he was also intimidated to play the character as he felt the role of Freddy belonged to Robert Englund.

This was the most expensive A Nightmare on Elm Street film to date with a budget of $35 million.

Despite fans not being overall pleased with it, this was the highest grossing remake to date.

DEVIL

Release Date	September 17, 2010
Budget	$10,000,000
Studio	Universal Pictures, Media Rights Capital, The Night Chronicles
Run Time	80 minutes
Sub-genre	Supernatural
Source / Inspiration	---
Writers	Brian Nelson, M. Night Shyamalan
Producers	M. Night Shyamalan, Sam Mercer
Directors	John Erick Dowdle
Box Office	$62,600,000
Awards	---

Main Cast	
Actor / Actress	**Screen Names**
Chris Messina	Detective Bowden
Logan Marshall-Green	Mechanic
Jenny O'Hara	Old Woman

Bojana Novakovic	Young Woman
Caroline Dhavernas	Elsa
Jacob Vargas	Ramirez
Facts / More	
This film as able to recoup its entire production budget in its opening weekend.	
This film was not screened for critics, supposedly to prevent the twist being shared with the public.	

LET ME IN

Release Date	October 1, 2010
Budget	$20,000,000
Studio	Overture Films, Relativity Media, Paramount Pictures, Icon Film Distribution, EFTI, Hammer Films, Exclusive Media Group
Run Time	116 minutes
Sub-genre	---
Source / Inspiration	Let the Right One In (Vampire Novel) by John Ajvide Lindqvist
Writers	Matt Reeves, John Ajvide Lindqvist
Producers	Alex Brunner, Simon Oakes, Guy East, Tobin Armbrust, Donna Gigliotti, John Nordling, Carl Molinder, EFTI, Hammer Films, Exclusive Media Group
Directors	Matt Reeves
Box Office	$24,100,000
Awards	Academy of Science Fiction, Fantasy & Horror Films, USA – Saturn Award
	Austin Film Critics Association – Breakthrough Artist Award
	Central Ohio Film Critics Association – COFCA Award
	Empire Awards, UK – Empire Award
	Fangoria Chainsaw Awards – Chainsaw Award
	Fright Meter Awards – Fright Meter Award
	IGN Summer Movie Awards – IGN Award
	National Board of Review, USA – NBR Award
	Phoenix Film Critics Society Awards – PFCS Award
	Scream Awards – Scream Award

Main Cast	
Actor / Actress	**Screen Names**
Kodi Smit-McPhee	Owen
Chloe Grace Moretz	Abby
Richard Jenkins	The Father
Cara Buono	Owen's Mother

Sasha Barrese	Virginia
Facts / More	

The morse code at the end of the trailer spells out "Help Me".

In the scene where Abby is bleeding in front of Owen because she wasn't invited in, she wears a KISS Destroyer T-shirt. In the original novel, the KISS Destroyer album was the first cassette Oskar (Owen) listens to after he buys a Sony Walkman.

I SPIT ON YOUR GRAVE

Release Date	October 8, 2010
Budget	$2,000,000
Studio	Anchor Bay Entertainment, Cinetel Films
Run Time	108 minutes
Sub-genre	Torture
Source / Inspiration	Remake
Writers	Adam Rockoff
Producers	Lisa M. Hansen, Paul Hertzberg, Cinetel Films
Directors	Steven R. Monroe
Box Office	$572,809
Awards	---

Main Cast	
Actor / Actress	**Screen Names**
Sarah Butler	Jennifer
Jeff Branson	Johnny
Andrew Howard	Scorch
Facts / More	

After casting was complete, the actors only had two weeks to rehearse.

PIRANHA 3D

Release Date	August 20, 2010
Budget	$24,000,000
Studio	The Weinstein Company, Dimension Films, Atmosphere Entertainment, Chako Film Company, Intellectual Properties Worldwide
Run Time	84 minutes
Sub-genre	---
Source / Inspiration	Remake
Writers	Pete Goldfinger, Josh Stolberg
Producers	Aleandre Aja, Mark Canton, Marc Toberoff, Gregory Levasseur, Dimension Films,

	Atmosphere Entertainment, Chako Film Company, Intellectual Properties Worldwide
Directors	Alexandre Aja
Box Office	$83,100,000
Awards	Olden Schmoes Awards – Golden Schmoes
	Scream Awards – Scream Award

Main Cast	
Actor / Actress	**Screen Names**
Elisabeth Shue	Jodie Forester
Jerry O'Connell	Derrick Jones
Richard Dreyfuss	Matt Boyd
Christopher Lloyd	Mr. Carl Goodman
Eli Roth	Wet T-Shirt Host
Steven R. McQueen	Jake Forester
Jessica Szohr	Kelly
Kelly Brook	Danni
Riley Steele	Crystal

Facts / More

One of the TV Spots was banned before it showed too much gore and revealed the end of the movie.

The production estimated that 75,000 gallons of fake blood was used each day of shooting.

Elisabeth Shue and Christopher Lloyd also starred together in Back to the Future Part II and III.

THE CABIN IN THE WOODS	
Release Date	April 13, 2012
Budget	$30,000,000
Studio	Lionsgate, Mutant Enemy Productions
Run Time	95 minutes
Sub-genre	Mystery
Source / Inspiration	---
Writers	Joss Wheadon, Drew Goddard
Producers	Joss Whedon, Mutant Enemy Productions
Directors	Drew Goddard
Box Office	$66,500,000
Awards	Academy of Science Fiction, Fantasy & Horror Films, USA – Saturn Award
	Bram Stoker Awards – Bram Stoker Award
	Fangoria Chainsaw Awards – Chainsaw Award
	Fright Meter Awards – Fright Meter Award
	Golden Schmoes Awards – Golden Schmoes Award
	Golden Trailer Awards – Golden Trailer
	IGN Summer Movie Awards - IGN Award, IGN People's Choice Awards
	Kansas City Film Critics Circle Awards – Vincent Koehler Award
	Online Film & Television Awards – OFTA Film Award
	Rondo Hatton Classic Horror Awards – Rondo Statuette

Main Cast

Actor / Actress	Screen Names
Kristen Connolly	Dana
Chris Hemsworth	Kurt
Anna Hutchinson	Jules
Fran Kranz	Marty
Amy Acker	Lin

Facts / More

Sigourney Weaver and Chris Hemsworth later starred in the Ghostbusters reboot.

Jamie Lee Curtis was considered for the role of The Director, but it ultimately went to Sigourney Weaver. Joss Wheadon was excited about this and was also excited to finally be involved in a film with a werewolf.

SCREAM 4

Release Date	April 15, 2011
Budget	$40,000,000
Studio	Dimension Films, Corvus Corax Productions, Outerbanks Entertainment, The Weinstein Company
Run Time	111 minutes
Sub-genre	Mystery
Source / Inspiration	Sequel
Writers	Kevin Williamson
Producers	Wes Craven, Iya Labunka, Kevin Williamson
Directors	Wes Craven
Box Office	$97,100,000
Awards	Golden Trailer Awards – Golden Trailer

Main Cast	
Actor / Actress	**Screen Names**
Neve Campbell	Sidney Prescott
Courtney Cox	Gale Weathers-Riley
David Arquette	Dewey Riley
Lucy Hale	Sherrie
Roger Jackson	Ghostface (voice)
Kristen Bell	Chloe

Facts / More

This was the last film directed by Wes Craven.

This film marks Scream as being one of the only horror franchises to have its director and main character return for all the sequels.

The movie opened 15 years to the day after Scream (1996) filming began.

SINISTER	
Release Date	October 12, 2012
Budget	$3,000,000
Studio	Summit Entertainment, Lionsgate, Momentum Pictures, Alliance Films, Automatik, Blumhouse Productions, IM Global
Run Time	109 minutes
Sub-genre	Supernatural
Source / Inspiration	---
Writers	Scott Derrickson, C. Robert Cargill
Producers	Jason Blum, Scott Derrickson, Alliance Films, Automatik, Blumhouse Productions, IM Global
Directors	Scott Derrickson
Box Office	$87,700,000
Awards	Fangoria Chainsaw Awards – Chainsaw Award
	Fright Meter Awards – Fright Meter Award
	Golden Trailer Awards – Golden Trailer

Main Cast	
Actor / Actress	**Screen Names**
Ethan Hawke	Ellison Oswalt
Juliet Rylance	Tracy

Facts / More

The family that was hanged on a tree were all played by stuntmen, however when the scene was first done the stunt coordinator botched the preparations for the scene resulting in the actors being legitimately hanged and choked. Fortunately they survived, and the coordinator was fired soon after.

There's very little blood, no swearing and no nudity because the film makers were going for a PG-13 rating, but they got an R-Rating based on the content alone.

THE LORDS OF SALEM	
Release Date	September 10, 2012 (TIFF), April 19, 2013
Budget	$1,500,000
Studio	Anchor Bay Films, Entertainment One, Haunted Movies
Run Time	101 minutes
Sub-genre	---
Source / Inspiration	---

Writers	Rob Zombie
Producers	Rob Zombie, Jason Blum, Andy Gould, Oren Peli, Haunted Movies
Directors	Rob Zombie
Box Office	$1,500,000
Awards	Fright Meter Awards – Fright Meter Award

Main Cast	
Actor / Actress	**Screen Names**
Sheri Moon Zombie	Heidi Hawthorne
Meg Foster	Margaret Morgan
Bruce Davison	Francis Matthias

Facts / More
There are no digital effects in this film.
Filmed in the actual town of Salem.

V/H/S

Release Date	October 5, 2012
Budget	$15,000
Studio	Magnet Releasing, Bloody Disgusting, The Collective
Run Time	116 minutes
Sub-genre	Found Footage
Source / Inspiration	---
Writers	Brad Miska, Simon Barrett, David Bruckner, Nicolas Tecowsky, Ti West, Glenn McQuaid
Producers	Simon Barrett, Gary Binkow, Brad Miska, Roxanne Benjamin, Bloody Disgusting, The Collective, Radio Silence
Directors	Matt Bettenelli-Olpin, David Bruckner, Tyler Gillett, Justin Martinez, Glenn McQuaid, Radio Silence, Joe Swanberg
Box Office	$1,900,000
Awards	---

Main Cast	
Actor / Actress	**Screen Names**
---	---

Facts / More
Tuesday the 17th would take place right after Friday the 13th. The name and camping ground was a nod to Friday the 13th.

SMILEY

Release Date	October 12, 2012
Budget	---
Studio	Fever Productions LLC, MIC Promotions, Level 10 Films
Run Time	95 minutes
Sub-genre	---
Source / Inspiration	---
Writers	Glasgow Philipps, Michael J. Gallagher, Ezra Cooperstein
Producers	Michael Wormser, Level 10 Films
Directors	Michael Gallagher
Box Office	---
Awards	---

Main Cast

Actor / Actress	Screen Names
Caitlin Gerard	Ashley
Melanie Papalia	Proxy
Shane Dawson	Binder
Andrew James Allen	Zane

Facts / More

The marketing team boasted about the film's trailer having over 30 million views, but the film allegedly only sold 30,000 copies. Some of the DVD artwork even had "30+ million trailer views" on a banner across the top of the artwork.

THE CONJURING

Release Date	July 19, 2013
Budget	$20,000,000
Studio	Warner Bros. Pictures, New Line Cinema, The Safran Company, Evergreen Media Group
Run Time	12 minutes
Sub-genre	Supernatural
Source / Inspiration	Ed & Lorraine Warren investigations
Writers	Chad Hayes, Carey W. Hayes
Producers	Tony DeRosa-Grund, Peter Safran, Rob Cowan, New Line Cinema, The Safran Company, Evergreen Media Group
Directors	James Wan
Box Office	$319,500,000
Awards	Academy of Science Fiction, Fantasy & Horror Films, USA – Saturn Award
	Empire Awards, UK – Empire Award
	Fnagoria Chainsaw Awards – Chainsaw Award
	Fright Meter Award – Fright Meter Award
	Golden Schmoes Awards – Golden Schmoes
	Golden Trailer Awards – Golden Trailer
	IGN Summer Movie Award – IGN Award
	Online Film & Television Association – OFTA Film Award
	Rondo Hatton Classic Horror Awards – Rondo Statuette

Main Cast

Actor / Actress	Screen Names
Patrick Wilson	Ed Warren
Vera Farmiga	Lorraine Warren
Ron Livingstone	Roger Perron
Lilli Taylor	Caroline Perron

Facts / More

The real Perron family visited the set of the film.

When the movie was shown in the Philippines, some cinemas had to hire Catholic priests to bless the viewers before showing it. This was due to some viewers having reported a "Negative Presence" after watching the film. The priests also provided spiritual and psychological help to the viewers.

The film contain no nudity, minimal blood, minimal profanity, no smoking and barely any alcohol content, but the film received an R-Rating simply because of its scare factor.

EVIL DEAD

Release Date	April 5, 2013
Budget	$17,000,000
Studio	Sony Pictures, TriStar Pictures, Ghost House Pictures, FilmDistrict
Run Time	92 minutes
Sub-genre	---
Source / Inspiration	Remake
Writers	Fede Alvarez, Rodo Sayagues, Sam Raimi
Producers	Robert Tapert, Sam Raimi, Bruce Campbell, TriStar Pictures, Ghost House Pictures, FilmDistrict
Directors	Fede Alvarez
Box Office	$97,500,000
Awards	Fangoria Chainsaw Awards – Chainsaw Award Fright Meter Awards – Fright Meter Award International Film Music Critics Awards – IFMCA Award Key Art Awards – Key Art Award

Main Cast	
Actor / Actress	**Screen Names**
Jane Levy	Mia
Jessica Lucas	Olivia
Shiloh Fernandez	David
Lou Taylor Pucci	Eric
Elizabeth Blackmore	Natalie

Facts / More
If you take the First letters of the five main characters, David, Eric, Mia, Olivia, Natalie, it spells "DEMON".

DARK SKIES

Release Date	February 22, 2013
Budget	$3,500,000
Studio	Dimension Films, The Weinstein Company, Alliance Films, IM Global, Blumhouse Productions, Robotproof
Run Time	97 minutes
Sub-genre	Extra-Terrestrials
Source / Inspiration	---
Writers	Scott Stewart

Producers	Jason Blum, Couper Samuelson, Jeanette Brill, Dimension Films, Alliance Films, IM Global, Blumhouse Productions, Robotproof
Directors	Scott Stewart
Box Office	$27,800,000
Awards	---

Main Cast	
Actor / Actress	**Screen Names**
Keri Russell	Lacy Barrett
Jake Brennan	Bobby Jessop
Josh Hamilton	Daniel Barrett

Facts / More
This film was originally pitched as a found footage movie.

WER

Release Date	November 16, 2013 (Japan), September 23, 2014
Budget	---
Studio	FilmDistrict, Sierra Pictures, Incentive Filmed Entertainment, Prototype, Room 101, Inc.
Run Time	93 minutes
Sub-genre	Supernatural
Source / Inspiration	---
Writers	William Brent Bell, Matthew Peterman
Producers	Matthew Peterman, Morris Paulson, Steven Schneider, FilmDistrict, Sierra Pictures, Incentive Filmed Entertainment, Prototype, Room 101, Inc.
Directors	William Brent Ball
Box Office	---
Awards	---

Main Cast	
Actor / Actress	**Screen Names**
A. J. Cook	Kate Moore
Brian Scott O'Connor	Talan Gwynek
Sebastian Roche	Klaus Pistor

Facts / More
Sebastian Roche's character in the film is "Klaus". This is also the name of a vampire/werewolf hybrid in The Vampire Diaries. Sebastian play's Klaus' father (Michael) in the series.
Filming began in 2012 in Bucharest, Romania, a location that was used in The New England Vampire book that also includes werewolves.

THE PURGE

Release Date	June 7, 2013
Budget	$3,000,000
Studio	Universal Pictures, Blumhouse Productions, Why Not Productions, Platinum Dunes, Dentsu, Overlord Productions
Run Time	85 minutes
Sub-genre	---
Source / Inspiration	---
Writers	James DeMonaco
Producers	Jason Blum, Michael Bay, Andrew Form, Brad Fuller, Sebastien K. Lemercier, Blumhouse Productions, Why Not Productions, Platinum Dunes, Dentsu, Overlord Productions
Directors	James DeMonaco
Box Office	$89,300,000
Awards	ASCAP Film & Television Music Awards – ASCAP Award Fright Meter Awards – Fright Meter Award

Main Cast	
Actor / Actress	**Screen Names**
Ethan Hawke	James Sandin
Lena Headey	Mary Sandin
Max Burkholder	Charlie Sandin
Adelaine Kane	Zoey Sandin

Facts / More
The idea came to James DeMonaco while he and his wife were driving and were cut off by a drunk driver. This resulted in them nearly dying. A fight broke out and police had to intervene. His wife said how great it would be to get one free murder a year. This was said to be the inspiration for the concept.

MAMA

Release Date	January 18, 2013
Budget	$15,000,000
Studio	Universal Pictures, Toma 78, De Milo Productions, Mist Entertainment
Run Time	100 minutes
Sub-genre	---
Source / Inspiration	Mama by Andy Muschietti
Writers	Andy Muschietti, Barbara Muschietti, Neil Cross
Producers	J. Miles Dale, Barbara Muschietti, Toma 78, De Milo Productions, Mist Entertainment
Directors	Andy Muschietti
Box Office	$146,400,000
Awards	ASCAP Film & Television Music Awards – SCAP Award

Directors Guild of Canada – DGC Craft Award

Fantasporto – International Fantasy Film Award

Golden Trailer Awards – Golden Trailer

Gerardmer Film Festival – Audience Award, Grand Prize, Youth Jury Grand Prize

Palm Springs International Film Festival – Directors to Watch

Main Cast	
Actor / Actress	**Screen Names**
Jessica Chastain	Annabelle
Nikolaj Coster-Waldau	Lucas
Megan Charpentier	Victoria
Javier Botet	Mama

Facts / More
Jessica Chastain was the first and only choice for the role of Annabelle.
Although the entire film was the creation of Andy Muschietti, he didn't return to direct the sequel becaue of his commitment to It (2017).

INSIDIOUS CHAPTER II

Release Date	September 13, 2013
Budget	$5,000,000
Studio	FilmDistrict, Sony Pictures, Blumhouse Productions, Stage 6 Films, Entertainment One
Run Time	106 minutes
Sub-genre	Supernatural
Source / Inspiration	Sequel
Writers	Leigh Whannell, James Wan
Producers	Jason Blum, Oren Peli, Blumhouse Productions, Stage 6 Films, Entertainment One
Directors	James Wan
Box Office	$161,900,000
Awards	---

Main Cast	
Actor / Actress	**Screen Names**
Patrick Wilson	Josh Lambert
Rose Byrne	Renai Lambert
Barbara Hershey	Lorraine Lambert
Lin Shaye	Elise Rainier

Facts / More
The Linda Vista Hospital in the film has featured in over 30 horror films and TV shows.

TEXAS CHAINSAW 3D

Release Date	January 4, 2013
Budget	$20,000,000
Studio	Lionsgate, Millennium Filmls, Mainline Pictures
Run Time	92 minutes
Sub-genre	Slasher
Source / Inspiration	Remake
Writers	Adam Marcus, Debra Sullivan, Kirsten Elms
Producers	Carl Mazzocone, Millennium Filmls, Mainline Pictures
Directors	John Luessonhop
Box Office	$47,200,000
Awards	Fangoria Chainsaw Awards – Chainsaw Award Golden Trailer Awards – Golden Trailer

Main Cast	
Actor / Actress	**Screen Names**
Alexandr Daddario	Heather Miller
Tania Raymonde	Nikki
Trey Songs	Ryan
Scott Eaastwood	Carl
Dan Yeager	Leatherface

Facts / More
The film ignores every every other Texas Chainsaw movie after the original. It is a direct sequel to Texas Chainsaw Massacre (1974).

HANSEL & GRETEL: WITCH HUNTERS

Release Date	January 25, 2013
Budget	$50,000,000
Studio	Paramount Pictures, MGM, MTV Films, Gary Sanchez Productions, Studio Babelsberg, Flynn Picture Company
Run Time	88 minutes
Sub-genre	Fantasy
Source / Inspiration	Hansel & Gretel by The Brothers Grimm
Writers	Tommy Wirkola
Producers	Will Ferrell, Beau Flynn, Adam McKay, Kevin Messick, MGM, MTV Films, Gary Sanchez Productions, Studio Babelsberg, Flynn Picture Company
Directors	Tommy Wirkola

Box Office	$226,300,000
Awards	3D Creative Arts Awards – Lumiere Award
	Golden Trailer Awards – Golden Trailer Award
	International 3D & Advanced Imaging Society's Creative Art Awards – 3D Creative Art Awards: Europe

Main Cast	
Actor / Actress	**Screen Names**
Jeremy Renner	Hansel
Gemma Arterton	Gretel
Famke Janssen	Muriel
Peter Stormare	Sheriff Berringer
Derek Meyers	Edward

Facts / More
Hansel shoots a hostage to get to the villain in this film. Jeremy Renner, who plays Hansel, does the same thing in the movie SWAT.

CARRIE

Release Date	October 18, 2013
Budget	$30,000,000
Studio	Sony Pictures, MGM, Screen Gems, Misher Films
Run Time	99 minutes
Sub-genre	---
Source / Inspiration	Remake, Stephen King's Carrie
Writers	Lawrence D. Cohen, Roberto Aguirre-Sacasa
Producers	Kevin Misher
Directors	Kimberley Pierce
Box Office	$84,800,000
Awards	Academy of Science Fiction, Fantasy & Horror Films, USA – Saturn Award
	Alliance of Women Film Journalists – EDA Special Mention Award
	Home Media Magazine Awards – Home Media Magazine Award
	People's Choice Awards, USA – People's Choice Award
	The Joey Awards, Vancouver – Joey Award
	Women Film Critics Circle Awards – WFCC Award

Main Cast	
Actor / Actress	**Screen Names**
Chloe Grace Moretz	Carrie White
Julianne Moore	Margaret Whit

| Gabriella Wilde | Sue Snell |

Facts / More

This is one of the only remakes of a remake. Carrie (1976), Carrie (2002), Carrie (2013).

The rocks that rain at the end of the film were real. Stunt doubles were used in order not to hurt the real actresses.

For the shattered mirror scene, the filmmakers tried to shoot it practically with the shards of glass being manipulated by wires. The results were unsatisfactory, so they employed CGI.

OCULUS

Release Date	September 8, 2013 (TIFF), April 11, 2014
Budget	$5,000,000
Studio	Relativity Media, Blumhouse Productions, WWE Studios, MICA Entertainment, Mist Entertainment, Intrepid Pictures
Run Time	103 minutes
Sub-genre	Supernatural
Source / Inspiration	*Oculus: Chapter 3 – The Man with the Plan* by Mike Flanagan
Writers	Mike Flanagan, Jeff Howard, Jeff Seidman
Producers	Marc D. Evans, Trevor Macy, Jason Blum
Directors	Mike Flanagan
Box Office	$44,000,000
Awards	Fangoria Chainsaw Awards – Chainsaw Award
	Fright Meter Awards – Fright Meter Award

Main Cast	
Actor / Actress	**Screen Names**
Karen Gillan	Kaylie Russell
Brenton Thwaites	Tim Russell
Katee Sackhoff	Marie Russell
Rory Cochane	Alan Russell

Facts / More

A number of studios were prepared to back Oculus since 2006 if it was shot as a found footage movie, but Flanagan refused.

Stephen King was said to have rally enjoyed this movie.

CURSE OF CHUCKY

Release Date	August 2, 2013
Budget	$2,800,000
Studio	Universal Studios, Universal 1440 Entertainment

Run Time	96 minutes
Sub-genre	Slasher
Source / Inspiration	Sequel
Writers	Don Mancini
Producers	David Kirschner
Directors	Don Mancini
Box Office	$3,800,000
Awards	Academy of Science Fiction, Fantasy & Horror Films, USA – Saturn Award

Main Cast	
Actor / Actress	**Screen Names**
Chantal Quesnelle	Sarah
Fiona Dourif	Nica
Brad Dourif	Charles Ray Lee (voice)
Danielle Bisutti	Barb

Facts / More
In this film, Brad Dourif who plays the voice of Chucky, recorded all of his lines in less than a day.

GREEN INFERNO

Release Date	September 8, 2013 (TIFF), September 25, 2015
Budget	$5,000,000
Studio	BH Tilt, High Top Releasing, Worldview Entertainment, Dragonfly Entertainment, Sobras International Pictures
Run Time	100 minutes
Sub-genre	---
Source / Inspiration	---
Writers	Eli Roth, Guillermo Amoedo
Producers	Christopher Woodrow, Molly Connors, Eli Roth, Miguel Asensio, Nicolas Lopez
Directors	Eli Roth
Box Office	$12,900,000
Awards	iHorror Awards – iHorror Award

Main Cast	
Actor / Actress	**Screen Names**
Lorenza Izzo	Justine
Ariel Levy	Alejandro
Kirby Bliss Blanton	Amy
Daryl Sabara	Lars
Sky Ferreira	Kaycee

<table>
<tr><td colspan="2" align="center">Facts / More</td></tr>
<tr><td colspan="2">Eli Roth shared that the tribe offerd a two year old child to the production designer as a "thank you". The offer was politely declined.

When the villagers were shown Cannibal Holocaust (1980), they thought it was a comedy. They'd never seen a movie before.

Almost every villager signed up to be in the film. Some were even made into crew members.</td></tr>
</table>

I SPIT ON YOUR GRAVE 2

Release Date	September 20, 2013
Budget	$2,000,000
Studio	Anchor Bay Films, CineTel Films
Run Time	106 minutes
Sub-genre	---
Source / Inspiration	Sequel / Remake
Writers	Neil Elman, Thomas Fenton
Producers	Lisa M. Hansen, Paul Hertzberg, CineTel Films
Directors	Steven R. Monroe
Box Office	$668,119
Awards	---

Main Cast	
Actor / Actress	**Screen Names**
Jemma Dallender	Katie Carter

Facts / More
The only film in the series to include human trafficking.

WOLF CREEK 2

Release Date	August 30, 2013 (VFF), February 20, 2014
Budget	$1,700,000
Studio	Roadshow Film Distributors, Duo Art Productions, Emu Creek Pictures
Run Time	106 minutes
Sub-genre	Thriller
Source / Inspiration	Sequel
Writers	Greg McLean, Aaron Sterns
Producers	Helen Leake, Greg McLean, Steve Topic
Directors	Greg McLean
Box Office	$4,700,000

Awards	Australian Screen Sound Guild – ASSG Award
	Nocturna Madrid International Fantastic Film Festival - Nocturna Best Acting Award, Nocturna Best Director Award, Nocturna Best Script Award

Main Cast	
Actor / Actress	**Screen Names**
John Jarrett	Mick Taylor
Ryan Corr	Paul Hammersmith

Facts / More
All the gore and vehicle effects were done practically without the use of CGI.

AS ABOVE, SO BELOW	
Release Date	August 29, 2014
Budget	$5,000,000
Studio	Universal Pictures, Legendary Pictures, Brothers Dowdle Productions
Run Time	93 minutes
Sub-genre	Supernatural
Source / Inspiration	Catacombs, France
Writers	John Erick Dowdle, Drew Dowdle
Producers	Thomas Tull, John Jashni, Drew Dowdle, Patrick Aiello
Directors	John Erick Dowdle
Box Office	$41,900,000
Awards	Golden Trailer Awards – Golden Trailer

Main Cast	
Actor / Actress	**Screen Names**
Perdita Weeks	Scarlett
Ben Feldman	George
Edwin Hodge	Benji
Francois Civil	Papillon

Facts / More
The film was actually filmed in the catacombs below the streets of Paris, not a movie set. This was the first ever production to be granted permission from the French government to film in the catacombs.

CLOWN	
Release Date	November 13, 2014 (Italy), June 17, 2016
Budget	$1,500,000
Studio	Dimension Films, Cross Creek Productions, PS 260, Vertebra Films, Zed Filmworks, Method Studios, Dragonfly Entertainment
Run Time	100 minutes
Sub-genre	---
Source / Inspiration	---
Writers	Christopher Ford, Jon Watts
Producers	Mac Cappuccino, Eli Roth, Cody Ryder
Directors	Jon Watts

Box Office	$2,100,000
Awards	---
Main Cast	
Actor / Actress	**Screen Names**
Andy Powers	Kent
Laura Allen	Meg
Peter Stormare	Karlsson
Facts / More	
The Italian movie poster was censored for being too scary.	

IT FOLLOWS

Release Date	May 17, 2014 (Cannes), March 13, 2015
Budget	$1,300,000
Studio	RadiUS-TWC, Northern Lights Films, Animal Kingdom, Two Flints
Run Time	100 minutes
Sub-genre	---
Source / Inspiration	---
Writers	David Robert Mitchell
Producers	Rebecca Green, Laura D. Smith, David Robert Mitchell, David Kaplan, Erik Rommesmo, Northern Lights Films, Animal Kingdom, Two Flints
Directors	David Robert Mitchell
Box Office	$23,300,000
Awards	Austin Fantastic Fest – Next Wave Award
	Bram Stoker Awards – Bram Stoker Award
	Deauville Film Festival – Critics Award
	Fangoria Chainsaw Awards – Chainsaw Award
	Fright Meter Awards – Fright Meter Award
	Golden Schmoes Awards – Golden Schmoes
	Gerard Film Festival – Critic's Prize, Grand Prize
	Hampton's International Film Festival – Breakthrough Performer
	Home Media Magazine Awards – Home Media Magazine Award
	Horror Society Awards – Horror Society Award
	IGN Summer Movie Awards – IGN Award, IGN People's Choice Award
	iHorror Awards – iHorror Award
	National Board of Review, USA – NBR Award
	Neuchatel International Fantastic Film Festival – Denis-de-Roguement Youth Award,

	International Critic's Award
	Nocturna Madrid International Fantastic Film Festival – Nocturna Audience Award, Best Movie
	Phoenix Critics Circle – PCC Award

Main Cast	
Actor / Actress	**Screen Names**
Maika Monroe	Jay Height
Keir Gilchrist	Paul
Olivia Luccardi	Yara
Lili Sepe	Kelly Height

Facts / More
Th film's concept derives from a reoccurring nightmare the director had of a predator stalking him.

ANNABELLE

Release Date	October 3, 2014
Budget	$6,500,000
Studio	Warner Bros. Pictures, New Line Cinema, RatPac-Dune Entertainment, Atomic Monster Productions, The Safran Company
Run Time	98 minutes
Sub-genre	Supernatural
Source / Inspiration	Sequel / Prequel
Writers	Gary Dauberman
Producers	Peter Safran, James Wan
Directors	John R. Leonetti, James Wan
Box Office	$257,600,000
Awards	IHorror Awards – iHorror Award

Main Cast	
Actor / Actress	**Screen Names**
Ward Horton	John
Annabelle Wallis	Mia
Alfre Woodard	Evelyn

Facts / More
The movie portrays the Annabelle doll as a porcelain doll, but the real Annabelle doll is a larger Raggedy Ann doll. The Warrens had a special case built for the Annabelle doll which still resides in their occult museum today and is considered extremely haunted.
The elevator scene was directed by James Wan.

FLIGHT 7500

Release Date	June 11, 2014 (Philippines), April 12, 2016
Budget	$5,000,000
Studio	CBS Films, Lionsgate, Vertigo Entertainment, Ozla Pictures, Ozla Productions
Run Time	97 minutes
Sub-genre	Supernatural
Source / Inspiration	---
Writers	Craig Rosenberg
Producers	Takashige Ichise, Roy Lee, Vertigo Entertainment, Ozla Pictures, Ozla Productions, CBS Films
Directors	Takashi Shimizu
Box Office	$2,800,000
Awards	---

Main Cast	
Actor / Actress	**Screen Names**
Leslie Bibb	Laura Baxter
Ryan Kwanten	Brad Martin
Amy Smart	Pia Martin
Jamie Chung	Suzy Lee

Facts / More

7500 is actually an aircraft transponder code to indicate a hi-jacking.

This film had multiple release dates and still doesn't have a US Blu-ray release.

OUIJA

Release Date	October 24, 2014
Budget	$8,000,000
Studio	Universal Pictures, Platinum Dunes, Blumhouse Productions, Hasbro Studios
Run Time	89 minutes
Sub-genre	Supernatural
Source / Inspiration	Ouija spirit boards
Writers	Juliet Snowdon, Stiles White
Producers	Michael Bay, Andrew Form, Bradley Fuller, Jason Blum, Bennett Schneir, Platinum Dunes, Blumhouse Productions, Hasbro Studios
Directors	Stiles White
Box Office	$103,600,000
Awards	Fangoria Chainsaw Awards – Chainsaw Award

<table>
<tr><td colspan="2" align="center">Main Cast</td></tr>
<tr><td>Actor / Actress</td><td>Screen Names</td></tr>
<tr><td>Olivia Cooke</td><td>Laine Morris</td></tr>
<tr><td>Ana Coto</td><td>Sarah Morris</td></tr>
<tr><td>Darren Kagasoff</td><td>Trevor</td></tr>
<tr><td>Bianca A. Santos</td><td>Isabelle</td></tr>
<tr><td colspan="2" align="center">Facts / More</td></tr>
<tr><td colspan="2">Despite popular belief of Ouija boards being banned in the UK, no ban has ever been imposed, they're just a little harder to acquire than in other countries like the US.</td></tr>
</table>

THE BABADOOK

Release Date	May 22, 2014
Budget	$2,000,000
Studio	Entertainment One, Umbrella Entertainment, Screen Australia, Causeway Films
Run Time	94 minutes
Sub-genre	Psychological Thriller
Source / Inspiration	Monster by Jennifer Kent
Writers	Jennifer Kent
Producers	Kristina Ceyton, Kristian Moliere, Screen Australia, Causeway Films
Directors	Jennifer Kent
Box Office	$10,300,000
Awards	Austin Fantastic Fest – Best Actor, Best Actress, Best Picture, Best Screenplay
	Austin Film Critics Association – Breakthrough Artist Award
	Australian Academy of Cinema & Television Arts – AACTA Award
	Australian Director's Guild – ADG Award
	Australian Film Critics Association Award – AFCA Award
	BloodGuts UK Horror Awards - BloodGuts UK Horror Award
	Bram Stoker Awards – Bram Stoker Award
	Bucheon International Fantastic Film Festival – Bucheon Choice Award
	Central Ohio Film Critics Association – COFCA Award
	Empire Awards, UK – Empire Award
	Fangoria Chainsaw Awards – Chainsaw Award
	Film Critics Circle of Australia Awards – FCCA Award
	Fright Meter Awards – Fright Meter Award
	Golden Schmoes Awards – Golden Schmoes
	Golden Trailer Awards – Golden Trailer

Gerardmer Film Festival – Audience Award, International Critics Award, Special Jury Prize, Youth Jury Grand Prize

Horror Society Awards – Horror Society Award

iHorror Awards – iHorror Award

Indiewire Critics' Poll – ICP Award

Kansas City Film Critics Circle Awards – Vincent Koehler Award

Las Vegas Film Critics Society Award – Sierra Award

New York Film Critics Circle Awards – NYFCC Award

North Carolina Film Critics Association – NCFCA Award

Puchon International Fantastic Film Festival – Best Actress

Sitges – Catalonian International Film Festival – Best Actress, Special Prize of the Jury

Toronto After Dark Film Festival – Special Award

Village Voice Film Poll – VVFP Award

Main Cast	
Actor / Actress	**Screen Names**
Essie Davis	Amelia Vanek
Noah Wiseman	Samuel
Daniel Henshall	Robbie

Facts / More
"Babadook" is an anagram for "a bad book".
Everyone who was alive at the beginning of the film was still alive at the end of the film, excluding the dog.

THE HOUSES OCTOBER BUILT

Release Date	October 10, 2014
Budget	---
Studio	Image Entertainment, RLJ Entertainment, Room 101, Foreboding Films
Run Time	91 minutes
Sub-genre	---
Source / Inspiration	---
Writers	Zack Andrews, Bobby Roe, Jason Zada
Producers	Zack Andrews, Steven Schneider, Room 101, Foreboding Films
Directors	Bobby Roe
Box Office	---
Awards	---
Main Cast	

Actor / Actress	Screen Names
Brandy Schaefer	Brandy
Zack Andrews	Zack
Bobby Roe	Bobby
Mikey Roe	Mikey
Facts / More	

KNOCK KNOCK

Release Date	October 9, 2016
Budget	$2,000,000
Studio	Lionsgate Premiere, Voltage Pictures, Camp Grey Productions, Dragonfly Entertainment, Sobras International Pictures
Run Time	99 minutes
Sub-genre	Thriller
Source / Inspiration	---
Writers	Eli Roth, Nicolas Lopez, Guillermo Amoedo
Producers	Eli Roth, Miguel Asensio, Colleen Camp, John T. DeGraye, Cassian Elwes, Micolas Lopez, Voltage Pictures, Camp Grey Productions, Dragonfly Entertainment, Sobras International Pictures
Directors	Eli Roth
Box Office	$6,3000,000
Awards	---

Main Cast	
Actor / Actress	**Screen Names**
Keanu Reeves	Evan
Lorenza Izzo	Genesis
Ana De Armas	Bell

Facts / More
Genesis writes on the mirror "it was NOT a dream", but the t-shirt she wears reads "it was all a dream".

CRIMSON PEAK

Release Date	October 16, 2015
Budget	$55,000,000
Studio	Universal Pictures, Legendary Pictures, Double Dare You Promotions
Run Time	119 minutes
Sub-genre	Supernatural
Source / Inspiration	---
Writers	Guillermo Del Toro, Matthew Robbins
Producers	Guillermo Del Toro, Callum Greene, Jon Jashni, Thomas Tull
Directors	Guillermo Del Toro
Box Office	$74,500,000

Awards	Academy of Science Fiction, Fantasy & Horror Films, USA – Saturn Award
	Fangoria Chainsaw Awards – Chainsaw Award
	Fright Meter Awards – Fright Meter Award
	The Joey Awards, Vancouver – Joey Award

Main Cast	
Actor / Actress	**Screen Names**
Mia Wasikowska	Edith Cushing
Jessica Chastain	Lucille Sharpe
Tom Hiddleston	Thomas Sharpe
Charlie Hunnam	Dr. Alan McMichael

Facts / More
Though the house was built in its entirety, it had to be ripped down after the movie to make space in the studio. Everything from the house was made. Nothing was salvaged or reused.

KRAMPUS

Release Date	December 4, 2015
Budget	$15,000,000
Studio	Universal Pictures, Legendary Pictures, Zam Pictures
Run Time	98 minutes
Sub-genre	Christmas
Source / Inspiration	Krampus from Austro-Bavarian folklore
Writers	Todd Casey, Michael Dougherty, Zach Shields
Producers	Thomas Tull, Jon Jashni, lex Garcia, Michael Dougherty, Legendary Pictures, Zam Pictures
Directors	Michael Dougherty
Box Office	$61,500,000
Awards	Fangoria Chainsaw Awards – Chainsaw Award
	Fright Meter Awards – Fright Meter Award
	iHorror Awards – iHorror Award
	International Film Music Critics Award – IFMCA Award

Main Cast	
Actor / Actress	**Screen Names**
Adam Scott	Tom
Toni Collette	Sarah
Allison Tolman	Linda
David Koecchner	Howard
Emjay Anthony	Max

<table>
<tr><td colspan="2" align="center">Facts / More</td></tr>
<tr><td colspan="2">The film was originally to release on November 25 but was pushed back to December 4 to coincide with the Krampusnacht, a traditional Austrian festival held on December 5 that celebrates the Krampus coming to punish naughty children.</td></tr>
</table>

AREA 51

Release Date	May 15, 2015
Budget	$5,000,000
Studio	Paramount Pictures, Insurge Pictures, Blumhouse Productions, IM Global, Incentive Filmed Entertainment, Solana Films, Room 101
Run Time	95 minutes
Sub-genre	Mystery
Source / Inspiration	---
Writers	Oren Peli, Christopher Denham
Producers	Jason Blum, Insurge Pictures, Blumhouse Productions, IM Global, Incentive Filmed Entertainment, Solana Films, Room 101
Directors	Oren Peli
Box Office	$7,556
Awards	---

Main Cast	
Actor / Actress	**Screen Names**
Reid Warner	Reid
Darrin Bragg	Darrin
Ben Rovner	Ben
Jelena Nik	Jelena

Facts / More
The house that is broken into seems to be the exact same house as that from Paranormal Activity 2.
The film was completed in 2009, but didn't get released in select theaters and on VOD until 2015.

INSIDIOUS CHAPTER III

Release Date	June 5, 2015
Budget	$11,000,000
Studio	Gramercy Pictures, Focus Features, Entertainment One Films, Sony Pictures, Blumhouse Productions, Entertainment One, Stage 6 Films
Run Time	98 minutes
Sub-genre	Supernatural
Source / Inspiration	Sequel
Writers	Leigh Whannell

Producers	Jason Blum, Oren Peli, James Wan
Directors	Leigh Whannell
Box Office	$113,000,000
Awards	Ihorror Awards – iHorror Award
	Palm Springs International Film Festival – Directors to Watch
	Young Entertainer Awards – Young Entertainer Award

Main Cast	
Actor / Actress	**Screen Names**
Dermot Mulroney	Sean Brenner
Stephanie Scott	Quinn Brenner
Angus Sampson	Tucker
Leigh Whannell	Specs

Facts / More
This film takes places in 2007, three years before Insidious and Insidious II.
The Wheezing Demon is the only antagonist who has not appeared once in the previous movies nor share any connection to the Lambert family.

GOODNIGHT MOMMY

Release Date	January 8, 2015
Budget	---
Studio	Stadtkino Verleih, Ulrich Seidl Film Produktion GmbH
Run Time	100 minutes
Sub-genre	---
Source / Inspiration	---
Writers	Veronika Franz, Severin Fiala
Producers	Ulrich Seidl, Ulrich Seidl Film Produktion GmbH
Directors	Veronika Franz, Severin Fiala
Box Office	$2,200,000
Awards	Austrian Film Awards, AT – Austrian Film Award
	Buenos Aires International Festival of Independent Cinema – ADF Cinematography Award
	Diagonale Austria – Diagonale Grand Prize
	European Film Awards – Carlo di Palma Award
	Fangoria Chainsaw Awards – Chainsaw Award
	Fantaspoa International Fantastic Film Festival – Jury Award
	Golden Trailer Awards – Golden Trailer

	Gerardmer Film Festival – Syfy Jury Award, Youth Jury Grand Prize
	Las Vegas Film Critics Society Awards – Sierra Award
	Ljubljana International Film Festival – KingFisher Award
	National Board of Review, USA – NBR Award
	Sitges – Catalonion International Film Festival – Grand Prize of European Fantasy Film Award in Silver, Special Mention, Melies d/Argent
	St. Louis Film Critics Association, US – SLFCA Award
	T-Mobile New Horizons International Film Festival, Poland – Audience Award
	Thessaloniki Film Festival – FIPRESCI Prize

Main Cast	
Actor / Actress	**Screen Names**
Lucas Schwarz	Lukas
Elias Schwarz	Elias
Susanne Wuest	Mutter

Facts / More
240 twins were auditioned for the main roles.
The actors were not given the script.

VATICAN TAPES

Release Date	July 24, 2015
Budget	$13,000,000
Studio	Lionsgate, Pantelion Films, H2F Entertainment, Lakeshore Entertainment
Run Time	91 minutes
Sub-genre	---
Source / Inspiration	---
Writers	Christopher Borrelli, Michael C. Martin, Chris Morgan
Producers	Chris Cowles, Gary Lucchesi, Chris Morgan, Tom Rosenberg, H2F Entertainment, Lakeshore Entertainment
Directors	Mark Neveldine
Box Office	$13,500,000
Awards	---

Main Cast	
Actor / Actress	**Screen Names**
Olivia Taylor Dudley	Angela
Michael Pena	Father Lozano
Dougray Scott	Roger
Djimon Hounsou	Vicar Imani

The screenplay for this film was featured in the 2009 Blacklist, a list of the "most liked" unmade scripts of the year.

THE WITCH

Release Date	February 19, 2016
Budget	$4,000,000
Studio	A24, Elevation Pictures, Universal Pictures, Parts & Labor, RT Features, Rooks Nest Entertainment, Maiden Voyage Pictures, Mott Street Pictures, Code Red Productions, Scythia Films, Pulse Films, Special Projects
Run Time	93 minutes
Sub-genre	---
Source / Inspiration	---
Writers	Robert Eggers
Producers	Rodrigo Teixeira, Daniel Bekerman, Lars Knudson, Jodi Redman, Jay Van Hoy, Parts & Labor, RT Features, Rooks Nest Entertainment, Maiden Voyage Pictures, Mott Street Pictures, Code Red Productions, Scythia Films, Pulse Films, Special Projects
Directors	Robert Eggers
Box Office	$40,400,000
Awards	Austin Fantastic Fest – Horror Jury Prize
	Austin Film Critics Association – AFCA Award
	BloodGuts UK Horror Awards – BloodGuts UK Horror Award
	Boston Society of Film Critics Awards – BSFC Award
	Bram Stoker Awards – Bram Stoker Award
	Chicago Film Critics Association Awards – CFCA Award
	Empire Awards, UK – Empire Award
	Fangoria Chainsaw Awards – Chainsaw Award
	Film Independent Spirit Awards – Independent Spirit Award
	Fright Meter Awards – Fright Meter Award
	Golden Trailer Awards – Golden Trailer
	Gotham Awards – Gotham Independent Film Award
	IGN Summer Movie Awards – IGN Award, IGN People's Choice Award
	Indiana Film Journalist's Association, US – IFJA Award
	Indiewire Critics' Poll – ICP Award
	International Cinephile Society Awards – ICS Award
	INOCA – Halfway Award
	Las Vegas Film Critics Society Awards – Sierra Award

	London Film Festival – Sutherland Award
	New Hampshire Film Festival – Best Feature
	New Mexico Film Critics – NMFC Award
	+++

Main Cast	
Actor / Actress	**Screen Names**
Anya-Taylor Joy	Thomasin
Ralph Ineson	William
Kate Dickie	Katherine
Julian Richings	Governor

Facts / More
The film was shot in only 25 days.
Most of the film's dialogue and lines were based on writings from the time.

THE LAZARUS EFFECT

Release Date	February 27, 2015
Budget	$3,300,000
Studio	Universal Pictures, Relativity Media, Lionsgate, Blumhouse Productions, Mossaic Media Group
Run Time	83 minutes
Sub-genre	Supernatural
Source / Inspiration	---
Writers	Luke Dawson, Jeremy Slater
Producers	Jason Blum, Jimmy Miller, Cody Zweig, Blumhouse Productions, Mossaic Media Group
Directors	David Gelb
Box Office	$38,400,000
Awards	---

Main Cast	
Actor / Actress	**Screen Names**
Olivia Wilde	Zoe
Mark Duplass	Frank
Evans Peters	Clay

Facts / More
"Zoe" is the Greek word for life.
The title comes from a Bible story in the Gospel of John, in the New Testament. Lazarus was a man who was resurrected by Jesus after being dead for four days.

POLTERGEIST

Release Date	May 22, 2015
Budget	$35,000,000
Studio	20th Century Fox, Fox 2000 Pictures, MGM, Ghost House Pictures, TSG Entertainment, Vertigo Entertainment
Run Time	93 minutes, 101 minutes (extended version)
Sub-genre	Supernatural
Source / Inspiration	Remake
Writers	David Lindsay-Abaire
Producers	Sam Raimi, Roy Lee, Robert Tapert, Fox 2000 Pictures, MGM, Ghost House Pictures, TSG Entertainment, Vertigo Entertainment
Directors	Gil Kenan
Box Office	$94,300,000
Awards	Fangoria Chainsaw Awards – Chainsaw Award

Main Cast	
Actor / Actress	**Screen Names**
Sam Rockwell	Eric Bowen
Rosemarie DeWitt	Amy Bowen
Saon Sharbino	Kendra Bowen
Kyle Catlett	Griffin Bowen
Kennedi Clements	Madison Bowen

Facts / More
Almost half the costumes and props were sold to a fan in England before the movie hit theaters.
This film was not screen in advance for critics.

I SPIT ON YOUR GRAVE 3: VENGEANCE IS MINE

Release Date	October 23, 2015
Budget	$2,000,000
Studio	Anchor Bay Films, CineTel Films
Run Time	91 minutes
Sub-genre	Torture
Source / Inspiration	Sequel
Writers	Daniel Gilboy
Producers	Lisa M. Hansen, Paul Hertzberg
Directors	R. D. Braunstein

Box Office	$144,420
Awards	---
Main Cast	
Actor / Actress	**Screen Names**
Sarah Butler	Jennifer Hills
Jen Landon	Marla
Doug McKeon	Oscar
Facts / More	

DON'T BREATHE	
Release Date	August 26, 2016
Budget	$9,900,000
Studio	Sony Pictures, Screen Gems, Stage 6 Films, Ghost House Pictures, Good Universe
Run Time	88 minutes
Sub-genre	Thriller
Source / Inspiration	---
Writers	Fede Alvarez
Producers	Fede Alvarez, Sam Raimi, Robert Tapert
Directors	Fede Alvarez
Box Office	$157,800,000
Awards	Academy of Science Fiction, Fantasy & Horror Films, USA – Saturn Award
	ASCAP Film & Television Music Awards - ASCAP Award
	Fangoria Chainsaw Awards – Chainsaw Award
	Fright Meter Awards – Fright Meter Award
	Golden Schmoes Awards – Golden Schmoes
	Golden Trailer Awards – Golden Trailer
	iHorror Awards – iHorror Award

Main Cast	
Actor / Actress	**Screen Names**
Stephen Lang	The Blind Man
Jane Levy	Rocky
Dylan Minnette	Alex
Daniel Zovatto	Money

Facts / More
In Brazil and South Korea, the film is called "Man in the Dark," which was the original English working title

THE FOREST	
Release Date	January 8, 2016
Budget	$10,000,000
Studio	Gramercy Pictures, Al-Film, Lava Bear Films
Run Time	93 minutes

Sub-genre	Supernatural
Source / Inspiration	Aokigahara Forest (Suicide Forest / Sea of Tress), Japan
Writers	Nick Antosca, Sarah Cornwell, Ben Katai
Producers	Tory Metzger, David S. Goyer, David Linde, AI-Film, Lava Bear Films
Directors	Jason Zada
Box Office	$37,600,000
Awards	Fangoria Chainsaw Awards – Chainsaw Award

Main Cast	
Actor / Actress	**Screen Names**
Natalie Dormer	Sara / Jess Price
Eoin Macken	Rob

Facts / More
Natalie Dormer went to Aokigahara Forest in Tokyo to do research. She went five meters off the path and took pictures. Her driver refused to go one inch off the path.

THE SHALLOWS

Release Date	June 24, 2016
Budget	$25,000,000
Studio	Sony Pictures, Colombia Pictures, Weimaraner Republic Pictures, Ombra Pictures
Run Time	86 minutes
Sub-genre	Thriller
Source / Inspiration	---
Writers	Anthony Jaswinski
Producers	Lynn Harris, Matti Lesham, Colombia Pictures, Weimaraner Republic Pictures, Ombra Pictures
Directors	Jaume Collett-Serra
Box Office	$119,100,000
Awards	Vega Digital Awards – Centauri Award

Main Cast	
Actor / Actress	**Screen Names**
Blake Lively	Nancy

Facts / More
Blake Lively was pregnant with her second child during filming.
Blake Lively admitted she as terrified of sharks and never saw Jaws (1975).
Blake Lively's orange bikini was a gift from fashion designer, Tory Burch.

SPLIT

Release Date	September 16, 2016 (Fantastic Fest), January 20, 2017
Budget	$9,000,000
Studio	Universal Pictures, Blinding Edge Pictures, Blumhouse Productions
Run Time	117 minutes
Sub-genre	Thriller
Source / Inspiration	---
Writers	M. Night Shyamalan
Producers	M. Night Shyamalan, Jason Blum, Marc Bienstock, Blinding Edge Pictures, Blumhouse Productions
Directors	M. Night Shyamalan
Box Office	$278,500,000
Awards	CinEuphoria Awards – CinEuphoria Fright Meter Awards – Fright Meter Award Golden Trailer Awards – Golden Trailer Hawaii Film Critics Society – HFCS Award The BAM Awards – The BAM Award Young Entertainers Awards – Young Entertainer Award

Main Cast

Actor / Actress	Screen Names
James McAvoy	Split (9 characters)
Anya Taylor-Joy	Casey Cooke
Betty Buckley	Dr. Karen Fletcher

Facts / More

Joauin Phoenix couldn't reach an agreement with production so the role went to James McAvoy.

LIGHTS OUT

Release Date	July 22, 2016
Budget	$4,900,000
Studio	Warner Bros. Pictures, New Line Cinema, RatPac-Dune Entertainment, Atomic Monster Productions, Grey Matter Productions
Run Time	81 minutes
Sub-genre	---
Source / Inspiration	Lights Out by David F. Sandberg
Writers	Eric Heissrer, David F. Sandberg
Producers	James Wan, Lawrence Grey, Eric Heisserer, New Line Cinema, RatPac-Dune Entertainment, Atomic Monster Productions, Grey Matter Productions

Directors	David F. Sandberg
Box Office	$148,900,000
Awards	Australian Cinematograph Society – NSW & ACT Silver Award
	iHorror Awards – iHorror Award
	Palm Springs International Film Festival – Directors to Watch

Main Cast	
Actor / Actress	**Screen Names**
Teresa Palmer	Rebecca
Gabriel Bateman	Martin
Maria Bello	Sophie
Billy Burke	Paul

Facts / More
This film made back its entire budget on opening day. This got the sequel an immediate green light.

THE CONJURING 2

Release Date	June 10, 2016
Budget	$40,000,000
Studio	Warner Bros. Pictures, New Line Cinema, The Safran Company, Atomic Monster Productions
Run Time	134 minutes
Sub-genre	Supernatural
Source / Inspiration	Sequel / Ed & Lorraine Warren investigations
Writers	Chad Hayes, Carey W. Hayes, James Wan
Producers	Peter Safran, Rob Cowan, James Wan
Directors	James Wan
Box Office	$321,300,000
Awards	ASCAP Film & Television Music Awards – ASCAP Award
	Golden Trailer Awards – Golden Trailer
	iHorror Awards – iHorror Award

Main Cast	
Actor / Actress	**Screen Names**
Vera Farmiga	Lorraine Warren
Patrick Wilson	Ed Warren
Madison Wolfe	Janet Hodgson
Frances O'Connor	Peggy Hodgson

Facts / More
A priest was brought in to bless the set on the first day of filming.

THE DARKNESS

Release Date	May 13, 2016
Budget	$4,000,000
Studio	BH Tilt, High Top Releasing, Blumhouse Productions, Chapter One Films, EMU Creek Pictures
Run Time	92 minutes
Sub-genre	---
Source / Inspiration	---
Writers	Greg McLean, Shayne Armstrong, S. P. Krause
Producers	Jason Blum, Matthew Kaplan, Bianca Martino, Blumhouse Productions, Chapter One Films, EMU Creek Pictures
Directors	Greg McLean
Box Office	$10,900,000
Awards	---

Main Cast	
Actor / Actress	**Screen Names**
Kevin Bacon	Peter Taylor
Radha Mitchell	Bronny Taylor
David Mazouz	Michael Taylor
Lucy Fry	Stephanie Taylor
Matt Walsh	Gary Carter

Facts / More
Parts of this film were shot on the bombing range in Melrose, New Mexico.

THE AXE MURDERS OF VILLISCA

Release Date	2016
Budget	---
Studio	---
Run Time	78 minutes
Sub-genre	Crime
Source / Inspiration	True Crime (Villisca murders)
Writers	Kevin Abrams, Owen Egerton, Tony E. Valenzuela
Producers	Seth Caplan, Michael Wormser
Directors	Tony E. Valenuela
Box Office	---
Awards	---

<table>
<tr><td colspan="2" align="center">Main Cast</td></tr>
<tr><td>Actor / Actress</td><td>Screen Names</td></tr>
<tr><td>Robert Adamson</td><td>Calen Hirsche</td></tr>
<tr><td>Jarrett Sleeper</td><td>Denny Shea</td></tr>
<tr><td>Alex Frnka</td><td>Jess</td></tr>
<tr><td colspan="2" align="center">Facts / More</td></tr>
<tr><td colspan="2">The true crimes of the Villisca house where six members of the Moore family and two guests were bludgeoned to death with an axe remains unsolved.</td></tr>
</table>

GET OUT

Release Date	February 24, 2017
Budget	$4,500,000
Studio	Universal Pictures, Blumhouse Productions, QC Entertainment, MonkeyPaw Productions
Run Time	104 minutes
Sub-genre	Thriller
Source / Inspiration	---
Writers	Jordan Peele
Producers	Sean McKittrick, Jason Blum, Edward H. Hamm Jr., Jordan Peele
Directors	Jordan Peele
Box Office	$255,400,000
Awards	Academy Awards, USA – Oscar +++

Main Cast	
Actor / Actress	**Screen Names**
Daniel Kaluuya	Chris Washington
Allison Williams	Rose Armitage
Bradley Whitford	Dean Armitage
Catherine Keener	Missy Armitage
Caleb Landry Jones	Jeremy Armitage

Facts / More
Get Out stayed in the top 10 for the first two months of release.
Highest grossing debut film to date for an original script.

IT

Release Date	September 8, 2017
Budget	$35,000,000
Studio	Warner Bros. Pictures, New Line Cinema, Lin Pictures, Vertigo Entertainment, KatzSmith Productions
Run Time	135 minutes
Sub-genre	Science Fiction
Source / Inspiration	Remake

Writers	Chase Palmer, Cary Joji Fukunaga, Gary Dauberman
Producers	Roy Lee, Dan Lin, Seth Grahame-Smith, David Katzenberg, Barbara Muschietti, New Line Cinema, Lin Pictures, Vertigo Entertainment, KatzSmith Productions
Directors	Andy Muschietti
Box Office	$701,800,000
Awards	Fright Meter Awards – Fright Meter Award
	Golden Schmoes Awards – Golden Schmoes
	Golden Trailer Awards – Golden Trailer
	IGN Summer Movie Awards – IGN People's Choice Award
	iHorror Awards – iHorror Award
	MTV Movie & TV Awards – MTV Movie & TV Award
	Odyssey Awards – Odyssey Award

Main Cast	
Actor / Actress	**Screen Names**
Jaeden Martell	Bill Denbrough
Jeremy Ray Taylor	Ben Hanscom
Sophia Lillis	Beverly Marsh
Finn Wolfhard	Richie Tozier

Facts / More
Pennywise only has four minutes of dialogue in the entire movie.
This film was shipped to theaters under the code name "POUND FOOLISH", which is a literal opposite of "PENNY WISE".

THE BYE BYE MAN

Release Date	January 13, 2017
Budget	$7,400,000
Studio	STX Entertainment, STXFilms, H. Brothers, Los Angeles Media Fund, Tang Media Productions, Intrepid Pictures
Run Time	96 minutes
Sub-genre	---
Source / Inspiration	---
Writers	Jonathan Penner
Producers	Trevor Macy, Jeffrey Soros, Simon Horsman, STXFilms, H. Brothers, Los Angeles Media Fund, Tang Media Productions, Intrepid Pictures
Directors	Stacy Title
Box Office	$29,900,0000
Awards	---

Main Cast

Actor / Actress	Screen Names
Douglas Smith	Elliot
Lucien Laviscount	John
Cressida Bonas	Sasha
Facts / More	
The film was completed over a year before its release.	

ANNABELLE: CREATION

Release Date	August 11, 2017
Budget	$15,000,000
Studio	Warner Bros. Pictures, New Line Cinema, Atomic Monster Productions, The Safran Company, RatPac-Dune Entertainment
Run Time	110 minutes
Sub-genre	Supernatural
Source / Inspiration	Sequel
Writers	Gary Dauberman
Producers	Peter Safran, James Wan
Directors	David F. Sandberg
Box Office	$306,500,000
Awards	---

Main Cast	
Actor / Actress	**Screen Names**
Anthony LaPaglia	Samuel Mullins
Samara Lee	Bee
Miranda Otto	Esther Mullins
Facts / More	

GERALD'S GAME

Release Date	September 29, 2017
Budget	---
Studio	Netflix
Run Time	103 minutes
Sub-genre	---
Source / Inspiration	Gerald's Game (novel) by Stephen King
Writers	Mike Flanagan, Jeff Howard

Producers	Trevor Macy
Directors	Mike Flanagan
Box Office	---
Awards	---

Main Cast	
Actor / Actress	**Screen Names**
Carla Gugino	Jessie
Bruce Greenwood	Gerald

Facts / More
Gerald refers to the dog as Cujo, which is in reference to another Stephen King novel.

CULT OF CHUCKY

Release Date	October 3, 2017
Budget	$6,500,000
Studio	Universal Pictures, Universal 1440 Entertainment
Run Time	91 minutes
Sub-genre	Slasher
Source / Inspiration	Sequel
Writers	Don Mancini
Producers	David Kirschner, Ogden Gavanski, Universal 1440 Entertainment
Directors	Don Mancini
Box Office	$2,200,000
Awards	---

Main Cast	
Actor / Actress	**Screen Names**
Brad Dourif	Chucky (voice)
Allison Dwaan Doiron	Rachel
Alex Vincent	Andy Barclay
Fiona Dourif	Nica Pierce

Facts / More
This film was shot in Canada.

LEATHERFACE

Release Date	October 20, 2017
Budget	---
Studio	Lionsgate, Campbell Grobman Films, Mainline Pictures, Millennium Films

Run Time	90 minutes
Sub-genre	Slasher
Source / Inspiration	Sequel
Writers	Seth M. Sherwood
Producers	Tobe Hooper, Christa Campbell, Lati Grobman, Carl Mazzocone, Les Weldon, Campbell Grobman Films, Mainline Pictures, Millennium Films
Directors	Julien Maurey, Alexandra Bustillo
Box Office	$1,500,000
Awards	---

Main Cast	
Actor / Actress	**Screen Names**
Stephen Dorff	Hal Hartman
Liili Taylor	Verna
Sam Strike	Jackson
Vanessa Grasse	Lizzy
Finn Jones	Deputy Sorells

Facts / More
This was the final film Tobe Hooper produced before his death.

CABIN 28

Release Date	2017
Budget	---
Studio	---
Run Time	123 minutes
Sub-genre	---
Source / Inspiration	True Crimes – The Keddie Murders
Writers	John Klyza
Producers	Lee Bane, Rebecca Graham, Andrew Jones
Directors	Andrew Jones
Box Office	---
Awards	---

Main Cast	
Actor / Actress	**Screen Names**
Terri Dwyer	Sue
Derek Nelson	Dana
Brendee Green	Sheila
Harriet Rees	Tina

Lee Bane	Marty
Facts / More	
Inspired by the true story of the Keddie Murders, an unsolved 1981 quadruple homicide that occurred in the town of Keddie in the USA. The murders took place in cabin 28 on the evening of April 11, 1981. The victims were Sue Sharp, her son John and his friend, Dana Wingate. After the crime was discovered Sue's daughter, Tina, was reported missing. Her skull was recovered in 1984 in Camp Eighteen, California.	

<table>
<tr><td colspan="2" align="center">A QUIET PLACE</td></tr>
<tr><td>Release Date</td><td>April 6, 2018</td></tr>
<tr><td>Budget</td><td>$22,000,000</td></tr>
<tr><td>Studio</td><td>Paramount Pictures, Platinum Dunes, Saturday Night Productions</td></tr>
<tr><td>Run Time</td><td>90 minutes</td></tr>
<tr><td>Sub-genre</td><td>Extra-Terrestrials</td></tr>
<tr><td>Source / Inspiration</td><td>---</td></tr>
<tr><td>Writers</td><td>Bryan Woods, Scott Beck, John Krasinski</td></tr>
<tr><td>Producers</td><td>Michael Bay, Andrew Form, Brad Fuller, Platinum Dunes, Saturday Night Productions</td></tr>
<tr><td>Directors</td><td>John Krasinski</td></tr>
<tr><td>Box Office</td><td>$350,300,000</td></tr>
<tr><td>Awards</td><td>Screen Actors Guild Awards – Actor

Academy of Science Fiction, Fantasy & Horror Films, USA – Saturn Award

AFI Awards, USA – AFI Award

Broadcast Film Critics Association Awards – Critics Choice Award

+++</td></tr>
<tr><td colspan="2" align="center">Main Cast</td></tr>
<tr><td>Actor / Actress</td><td>Screen Names</td></tr>
<tr><td>Emily Blunt</td><td>Evelyn Abbott</td></tr>
<tr><td>John Krasinski</td><td>Lee Abbott</td></tr>
<tr><td>Millicent Simmonds</td><td>Regan Abbott</td></tr>
<tr><td>Noah Jupe</td><td>Marcus Abbott</td></tr>
<tr><td colspan="2" align="center">Facts / More</td></tr>
<tr><td colspan="2">The film makers purchased twenty tons of corn and hired farmers to grow it for the set.</td></tr>
<tr><td colspan="2">The movie only contains around 25 lines of dialogue.</td></tr>
</table>

<table>
<tr><td colspan="2" align="center">THE STRANGERS: PREY AT NIGHT</td></tr>
<tr><td>Release Date</td><td>March 9, 2018</td></tr>
<tr><td>Budget</td><td>$5,000,000</td></tr>
<tr><td>Studio</td><td>Aviron Pictures, The Fyzz Facility, White Comet Films, BLOOM, Rogue Pictures</td></tr>
<tr><td>Run Time</td><td>85 minutes</td></tr>
<tr><td>Sub-genre</td><td>---</td></tr>
</table>

Source / Inspiration	Sequel
Writers	Bryan Bertino, Ben Ketai
Producers	Wayne Marc Godfrey, Mark Lane, Robert Jones, Ryan Kavanaugh, The Fyzz Facility, White Comet Films, BLOOM, Rogue Pictures
Directors	Johannes Roberts
Box Office	$32,100,000
Awards	---

Main Cast	
Actor / Actress	**Screen Names**
Christina Hendricks	Cindy
Martin Henderson	Mike
Bailee Madison	Kinsey
Lewis Pullman	Luke

Facts / More
There's a scene in the movie where Luke puts down a pistol on top of a book. The title of the book was "A Stranger is Watching."

HALLOWEEN

Release Date	October 19, 2018
Budget	$15,000,000
Studio	Universal Pictures, Miramax, Blumhouse Productions, Trancas International Films, Rough House Pictures
Run Time	106 minutes
Sub-genre	Slasher
Source / Inspiration	Sequel
Writers	Jeff Fradley
Producers	Malek Akkad, Jason Blum, Bill Block
Directors	David Gordon Green
Box Office	$255,600,000
Awards	Academy of Science Fiction, Fantasy & Horror Films, USA – Saturn Award Fright Meter Awards – Fright Meter Award Rondo Hatton Classic Horror Awards – Rondo Statuette

Main Cast	
Actor / Actress	**Screen Names**
Jamie Lee Curtis	Laurie Strode
James Jude Courtney	The Shape / Michael Myers
Judy Greer	Karen
Andi Matichak	Allyson

<table>
<tr><td colspan="2" align="center">Facts / More</td></tr>
<tr><td colspan="2">Jake Gyllenhaal helped convince Jamie Lee Curtis to reprise her role of Laurie Strode for the film. Jake Gyllenhaal is a family friend of Curtis' and is dubbed by her as an unofficial godson.</td></tr>
</table>

THE NUN

Release Date	September 7, 2018
Budget	$22,000,000
Studio	Warner Bros. Pictures, New Line Cinema, Atomic Monster Productions, The Safran Company
Run Time	96 minutes
Sub-genre	Supernatural
Source / Inspiration	Sequel / Prequel
Writers	Gary Dauberman
Producers	Peter Safran, James Wan, New Line Cinema, Atomic Monster Productions, The Safran Company
Directors	Corin Hardy
Box Office	$365,600,000
Awards	Golden Trailer Awards – Golden Trailer
	Hawaii Film Critics Society – HFCS Award

Main Cast	
Actor / Actress	**Screen Names**
Demian Bichir	Father Burke
Taissa Farmiga	Sister Irene
Jonas Bloquet	Frenchie
Bonnie Aarons	The Nun
Ingrid Bisu	Sister Oana
Patrick Wilson	Ed Warren
Vera Farmiga	Lorraine Warren

<table>
<tr><td colspan="2" align="center">Facts / More</td></tr>
<tr><td colspan="2">The film was shot entirely in Romania.</td></tr>
<tr><td colspan="2">The highest grossing movie in The Conjuring universe to date. And the shortest at 93 minutes.</td></tr>
</table>

SLENDER MAN

Release Date	August 10, 2018
Budget	$28,000,000
Studio	Sony Pictures, Screen Gems, Mythology Entertainment, Madhouse Entertainment, It Is No Dream Entertainment

Run Time	91 minutes
Sub-genre	---
Source / Inspiration	---
Writers	David Birke
Producers	Bradley J. Fischer, James Vanderbilt, William Sherak, Robyn Meisinger, Sarah Snow, Screen Gems, Mythology Entertainment, Madhouse Entertainment, It Is No Dream Entertainment
Directors	Sylvain White
Box Office	$51,700,000
Awards	---

Main Cast	
Actor / Actress	**Screen Names**
Joey King	Wren
Julia Goldani Telles	Hallie
Jaz Sinclair	Chloe
Annalise Basso	Katie

Facts / More
Movie theaters in most areas of Wisconsin refused to show this movie, saying that it was insensitive to the little girl and her family, even though the movie was not a portrayal of actual events.

SUMMER OF '84

Release Date	August 10, 2018
Budget	---
Studio	Gunpowder & Sky, Brighthouse Pictures
Run Time	106 minutes
Sub-genre	---
Source / Inspiration	---
Writers	Matt Leslie, Stephen J. Smith
Producers	Sean Williamson, Jameson Parker, Matt Leslie, Van Toffler, Cody Zweig, Gunpowder & Sky, Brighthouse Pictures
Directors	Francois Simard, Anouk Whissell, Yoann-Karl Whissell
Box Office	---
Awards	---

Main Cast	
Actor / Actress	**Screen Names**
Graham Verchere	Davey Armstrong
Judah Lewis	Tommy Eaton
Caleb Emery	Dale Woodworth

One of the photos of the missing boys shown is that of a victim of John Wayne Gacy.

IT: CHAPTER TWO

Release Date	September 6, 2019
Budget	$79,000,000
Studio	Warner Bros. Pictures, New Line Cinema, Double Dream, Vertigo Entertainment, Rideback
Run Time	170 minutes
Sub-genre	Fantasy
Source / Inspiration	Sequel / Remake / Stephen King
Writers	Gary Dauberman
Producers	Barbara Muschietti, Dan Lin, Roy Lee, New Line Cinema, Double Dream, Vertigo Entertainment, Rideback
Directors	Andy Muschietti
Box Office	$473,100,000
Awards	---

Main Cast	
Actor / Actress	**Screen Names**
Jessica Chastain	Beverly Marsh
James McAvoy	Bill Denbrough
Bill Hader	Richie Tozier

Facts / More
Jessica Chastain was considered for the role of Beverly before the first film had finished production. She was the first cast for the sequel.

ANNABELLE COMES HOMES

Release Date	June 26, 2019
Budget	$32,000,000
Studio	Warner Bros. Pictures, New Line Cinema, Atomic Monster Productions, The Safran Company
Run Time	106 minutes
Sub-genre	Supernatural
Source / Inspiration	Sequel
Writers	Gary Dauberman
Producers	James Wan, Peter Safran, New Line Cinema, Atomic Monster Productions, The Safran Company
Directors	Gary Dauberman

Box Office	$231,300,000
Awards	---

Main Cast	
Actor / Actress	**Screen Names**
Vera Farmiga	Lorraine Warren
Patrick Wilson	Ed Warren
McKenna Grace	Judy Warren
Madison Iseman	Mary Ellen

Facts / More
This movie is dedicated to Lorraine Warren who passed away two months before the release.

CHILD'S PLAY

Release Date	June 21, 2019
Budget	$10,000,000
Studio	United Artists Releasing, Elevation Pictures, Orion Pictures, Katzsmith Productions, Bron Creative
Run Time	90 minutes
Sub-genre	Slasher
Source / Inspiration	Child's Play / Chucky series
Writers	Tyler Burton Smith
Producers	David Katzenberg, Seth Grahame-Smith, Orion Pictures, Katzsmith Productions, Bron Creative
Directors	Lars Klevberg
Box Office	$45,000,000
Awards	Hawaii Film Critics Society – HFCS Award Leo Awards - Leo

Main Cast	
Actor / Actress	**Screen Names**
Tim Matheson	Henry Kaslan
Ben Daon	Ben
Zahra Anderson	Mom

Facts / More
At one point a toy police car is activated and states "dead or alive, you're coming with me." This is an obvious reference to Robocop, which was also released by Orion Pictures.

HAUNT

Release Date	September 13, 2019
Budget	---
Studio	Momentum Pictures, Sierra Affinity, Broken Road Productions, Nickel City Pictures
Run Time	92 minutes
Sub-genre	---
Source / Inspiration	---
Writers	Scott Beck, Bryan Woods
Producers	Todd Garner, Mark Fasano, Vishal Rungta, Ankur Rungta, Eli Roth, Sierra Affinity, Broken Road Productions, Nickel City Pictures
Directors	Scott Beck, Bryan Woods
Box Office	$2,400,000
Awards	---

Main Cast	
Actor / Actress	**Screen Names**
Katie Stevens	Harper
Will Brittain	Nathan
Shazi Raja	Angela
Lauryn Alisa Mclain	Bailey

Facts / More
Filmed in Fort Thomas, Kentucky, USA.

CRAWL

Release Date	July 12, 2019
Budget	$15,000,000
Studio	Paramount Pictures, Raimi Productions, Fire Axe Pictures
Run Time	87 minutes
Sub-genre	---
Source / Inspiration	---
Writers	Michael Rasmussen, Shawn Rasmussen
Producers	Craig Flores, am Raimi, Alexandre Aja, Raimi Productions, Fire Axe Pictures
Directors	Alexandre Aja
Box Office	$91,500,000
Awards	---

Main Cast	
Actor / Actress	**Screen Names**
Kaya Scodelario	Haley

Barry Pepper	Dave
Ross Anderson	Wayne
Facts / More	
This film had no press screenings.	

DOCTOR SLEEP

Release Date	November 8, 2019
Budget	$55,000,000
Studio	Warner Bros. Pictures, Intrepid Pictures, Vertigo Entertainment
Run Time	152 minutes
Sub-genre	---
Source / Inspiration	Doctor Sleep (novel) by Stephen King
Writers	Mike Flanagan
Producers	Trevor Macy, Jon Berg, Intrepid Pictures, Vertigo Entertainment
Directors	Mike Flanagan
Box Office	$72,300,000
Awards	Fangoria Chainsaw Awards – Chainsaw Award
	Fright Meter Awards – Fright Meter Award

Main Cast	
Actor / Actress	**Screen Names**
Ewan McGregor	Dan Torrence
Rebecca Ferguson	Rose the Hat
Kyleigh Curran	Abra Stone
Facts / More	

"You're gonna take your medicine" is a phrase often repeated when Jack Torrance threatens Danny in the novel The Shining.

PARASITE

Release Date	November 8, 2019
Budget	$15,500,000
Studio	CJ Entertainment, Barunson E&A
Run Time	132 minutes
Sub-genre	---
Source / Inspiration	---
Writers	Bong Joon Ho, Jin-Won Han
Producers	Kwak Sin-ae, Moon Yang-kwon, Bong Joon Ho, Jng Young-hwan, Barunson E&A

Directors	Bong Joon Ho
Box Office	$258,800,000
Awards	Academy Awards, USA – Oscar
	BAFTA Awards – BAFTA Award
	+++

Main Cast	
Actor / Actress	**Screen Names**
Kang-ho Song	Ki Taek
Sunkyun Lee	Doug Ik
Yeo-jeong Cho	Yeon Kyo
Woo-sik Choi	Ki Woo

Facts / More

2020

HOST	
Release Date	July 30, 2020
Budget	---
Studio	Vertigo Releasing, Shadowhouse Films
Run Time	56 minutes
Sub-genre	---
Source / Inspiration	---
Writers	Gemma Hurley, Rob Savage, Jed Shepherd
Producers	Douglas Cox, Craig Engler, Emily Gotto, Samuel Zimmerman, Shadowhouse Films
Directors	Rob Savage
Box Office	---
Awards	---

Main Cast	
Actor / Actress	**Screen Names**
Haley Bishop	Haley
Jemma Moore	Jemma
Emma Louise Webb	Emma
Radina Drandova	Radina

Facts / More
This film was filmed entirely on Zoom during the pandemic.
In order to get the cast worked up before certain takes the director would make them watch horror movie clips.

GRETEL & HANSEL	
Release Date	January 31, 2020
Budget	$5,000,000
Studio	United Artists, Orion Pictures, Automatik Entertainment, Bron Creative
Run Time	87 minutes
Sub-genre	Fantasy
Source / Inspiration	---
Writers	Rob Hayes
Producers	Brian Kavanaugh-Jones, Fred Berger
Directors	Oz Perkins

Box Office	$22,100,000
Awards	CinEuphoria Awards – CinEuphoria
	The BAM Awards – The BAM Award

Main Cast	
Actor / Actress	**Screen Names**
Sophia Lillis	Gretel
Samuel Leakey	Hansel
Alice Krige	The Witch
Jessica De Gouw	The Witch

Facts / More
At one point the witch in this movies says "What a world." Fans of the film The Wizard of Oz will recognize this as the Wicked Witch of the West's final words as she melts. The director of Gretel & Hansel, Osgood Perkins, often shortens his first name to Oz.

THE DARK AND THE WICKED

Release Date	November 6, 2020
Budget	---
Studio	RLJE Films, Unbroken Pictures, The Traveling Picture Show Company, Inwood Road Films
Run Time	93 minutes
Sub-genre	---
Source / Inspiration	---
Writers	Bryan Bertino
Producers	Bryan Bertino, Adrienne Briddle, Sonny Mallhi, Kevin Matusow, Unbroken Pictures, The Traveling Picture Show Company, Inwood Road Films
Directors	Bryan Bertino
Box Office	$422,174
Awards	---

Main Cast	
Actor / Actress	**Screen Names**
Marin Island	Louise Straker
Michael Abbott Jr.	Michael Straker
Julie Oliver-Touchstone	Virginia Straker
Lynn Andrews	Nurse

Facts / More
This was filmed at the director's family farm.

THE GRUDGE

Release Date	January 3, 2020
Budget	$14,000,000
Studio	Sony Pictures, Screen Gems, Stage 6 Films, Ghost House Pictures
Run Time	94 minutes
Sub-genre	Fantasy
Source / Inspiration	Remake . Sequel
Writers	Nicolas Pesce, Jeff Buhler
Producers	Sam Raimi, Robert Tapert, Takashige Ichise, Screen Gems, Stage 6 Films, Ghost House Pictures
Directors	Nicolas Pesce
Box Office	$49,500,000
Awards	---

Main Cast

Actor / Actress	Screen Names
Tara Westwood	Fiona Landers
Junko Bailey	Kayako Ghost
David Lawrence Brown	Sam Landers
Zoe Fish	Melinda Landers

Facts / More

The original plan was to reboot the series completely, featuring a new storyline that abandons the Saeki family. However, it was confirmed in an interview with Nicholas Pesce that the film takes place during the events of The Grudge (2004) and The Grudge 2 (2006).

THE INVISIBLE MAN

Release Date	February 28, 2020
Budget	$7,000,000
Studio	Universal Pictures, Blumhouse Productions, Goalpost Pictures, Nervous Tick Productions
Run Time	124 minutes
Sub-genre	---
Source / Inspiration	The Invisible Man by H. G. Wells
Writers	Leigh Whannell
Producers	Jason Blum, Kylie du Fresne, Blumhouse Productions, Goalpost Pictures, Nervous Tick Productions
Directors	Leigh Whannell
Box Office	$143,200,000
Awards	Austin Film Critics Association – AFCA Award AACTA Awards – AACTA Award

Australia Screen Editors – ASE Award

Bram Stoker Awards – Bram Stoker Award

Fangoria Chainsaw Awards – Chainsaw Award

+++

Main Cast	
Actor / Actress	**Screen Names**
Elisabeth Moss	Cecilia Kass
Oliver Jackson-Cohen	Adrian Griffin
Harriet Dyer	Emily Kass
Aldis Hodge	James Lanier
Facts / More	

The first name of the main character, Cecilia, is derived from the Latin Caecus which means blind or eyeless, Appropriately, she cannot see the Invisible Man. She is frequently called 'C' in the film, which, obviously, is pronounced like 'see.'

The password at Adrian's door is 1933, that was the year when the original film was released.

MORE AT STOCKROOMDEALS.COM

STOCKROOMDEAL$

www.ingramcontent.com/pod-product-compliance
Lightning Source LLC
Chambersburg PA
CBHW072242260726
48657CB00001BA/29